almost
innocent

DANCING IN THE SPACE BETWEEN

Michael Mish

For information contact:

Vesica Media
info@almost-innocent.com
Michael Mish
PO Box 3477 Ashland, OR 97520

DEDICATION

To the mavericks
To my parents
To all those thinking outside of the box

TABLE OF CONTENTS

The Loss of Innocence

ACKNOWLEDGMENTS

Thanks to those who have inspired me. Can anyone do better in a lifetime than to have inspired another person?

Thanks to Donna, Elspeth, Ryan, Mark, Linda and Jennifer for being there so we can remind each other that everything's going to be alright.

Thanks to Jean Liedloff, Bruce Lipton and Elena Vladimorova for their cutting edge insights.

Thanks to Chopin, Khachaturian, Brahms, Beethoven, Schubert, Humperdinck, Sibelius and Bach for always being there when I needed them most.

~

We come into this world and are innocent, then we take on all the conventions, social mores and beliefs of our culture
and mysteriously -- the innocence is gone.
I wanted to find out at what point I actually lost the wonder that comes with innocence and what it would take to get it back. This book is about my personal investigation after selling or giving away everything I owned in the name of reclaiming, what I would deem to be, the most important thing I've ever had:
the innocence I was born with.

Cover design by Richard Sisk
Graphic on this page by Jim Marin
Travel photos by Michael Mish

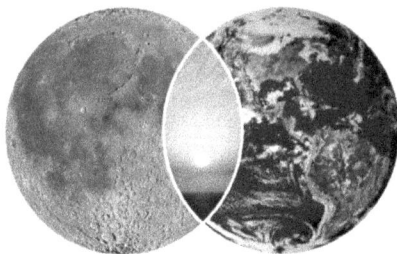

About the book

Exploring the dimly lit halls of my memory and the various minefields of childhood, I was struck by a joke that my brother and I still kid about:

"The whip."

"No, no. Anything but de whip."

"The whip."

"No, please. Anything but de whip."

"A-nyyyy thinnnng??"

(long pause, then with resignation...)

"De whip."

Depending on the delivery, timing and characterization one of us used, the 'joke' would have us crying with laughter. It is curious though. Within the joke's context, the known quantity – the whip – is preferable to the unknown...the unimaginable...the mystery. Our imaginations ran wild with what "anything" might entail. The invitation to the world of "anything", in childhood, was at once ubiquitous and forbidden.

The book you hold in your hand is about the journey of a life. Part 1 is a retrospective on my own life. I feel that, to a greater or lesser degree, all our experiences are universal experiences. So I hold up my life as an example of what happens to us all. Our personalities are forged in the crucible of change. And, more certain than anything else in life, change assures us that we will have joys and disappointments; wind and the rain; and we will regard these things as the stuff that simply happens in our lives. The qualities that we ascribe to these otherwise neutral events, and how we react to them, define who we are as people. Since I was a child I wanted to know who I was if all the events in my life were erased.

Many compromises were made to fit into a social system I neither enjoyed nor understood.

Part 2 deals with some of the insights I've come to, with regard to how we lose our innocence and how we can get it back. And, how 'anything' is far better than 'de whip'.

Reflections

Drunk with Dragonflies

Fremantle, W. Australia – January 2012

Lying on a broad green strip of grass, between the parking lot and the beach, I watched as a 3 year old boy looked toward the impossibly blue sky. It was already an unusually warm day on this early morning after my swim. His parents busied themselves with his younger brother as he fidgeted and protested at not being able to join his older brother orbiting freely around the family seated beneath the shade of a gum tree. The 3 year old marched on the grass bouncing his body as he beheld something that had one hundred percent of his attention. I glanced upward to see what he was looking at:

Dozens of dragonflies, alternately, hovering and darting just overhead.

The sun reflecting off their delicate gossamer wings, one of them played just above the boy's head as if teasing him. He followed the rainbow-winged insect bounce-walking as if in a trance. Wonder, uniquely relegated to the world of children and puppies, had him wheeling around like a marionette on rubberized strings. A giggle of delight hid just behind his expectant and smiling face. He tripped and tumbled as he followed the random dragonfly flight path. His world was the dragonflies. He didn't know where he ended and the dragonflies began. Was *he*, too, now a dragonfly?

"Look," he grunted at his parents pointing to the dragonfly still tantalizingly close but maddeningly out of reach.

"Dragonfly," his parents said.

"Dratchinfie?" he asked.

"Dragonfly," they repeated calmly.

He turned from his parents. The word didn't matter. What did matter, however, was the fascinating and seeming random flight trajectory of this insect that knew something special about the air. And it glanced off the air as the boy bobbed on the soft grass beneath his feet as he walked.

For him, the sky was a swirling mystical experience.

Nothing else existed for him. Just this new and magical discovery in the sky.

Of Princesses, Horses and Super Heroes

Yverdon, Switzerland August 2011

I spent the day at the beach yesterday. I was relaxing on the very used sand at a family lake-side littoral next to Lake Neuchatel where I am now, in the French part of Switzerland. The Jura Mountains rose like behemoth sentinels to my back and the alps sat implacably and mirage-like in the distance in what had become a hazy afternoon sky. One of the few picture-perfect places in the world, Switzerland was a place I always loved returning to. On this day at the lakeside beach there were two types of people:

People enjoying the warm sun and exquisite scenery

and

Princesses, horses and super heroes

The people were alternately swimming, eating or sunning themselves.

The children were doing something altogether different.

—

A 4 year old girl was completely immersed in a world she'd conceived in the sand. Most adults didn't notice that there was a protective bubble around her. She was separate and apart from all that was going on around her. With a peaceful self-possession about her, she had fashioned a world that was completely of her own making. Never once looking up to check out the activity around her, she hummed to herself as a beautiful woodland area sprung up around an enchanted castle immediately surrounded by an idly flowing moat. Elaborate walls fortified the castle that protected the rarefied beauty of the princess within. *She* was that princess combing her long amber locks in front of a mirror hung near a wooden stool where she sat. In her lofty chamber high above the castle walls, she surveyed an endless forested glade. She was both the creator of this sand universe and she was the universe itself. The rest of the world did not exist.

The rest of the world did not exist.

~

Another 5 year galloped through the sand, her blond mane dancing in the wind. She was an elegant and stunning horse with quick reflexes and an agile gait. There was no mistaking. She believed it so fully, that I saw the horse that she was. A beautiful white horse weaving between the people lying on their towels that were completely oblivious to the grace and beauty of this magnificent steed. There was majesty in the way the sun glinted off of its healthy coat.

There was nothing around her save for a few other horses. Other horses, that when they galloped swiftly enough, they flew. They flew between clouds and lit softly back on the ground when they found a suitable green field or, as was in this case, a suitable sandy beach. Not unlike the 4 year old girl hand-crafting her sand castle, the white horse provided its own orchestral musical score with sweeping strings and pulsing french horns against an incomparable landscape of endless dunes and blue, blue sky. As the white horse imagined new landscapes, so they were created. They were created instantly with the sublime beauty of an artist because this horse was the creator of its universe. It was one with its universe.

The rest of the world did not exist.

—

A 6-year-old boy was lobbing fireballs at one of the more menacing of the 'transformers'. And this transformer was a formidable opponent because he electrified his victims with a deft chop to the flanks. The fireball-throwing boy was a warrior. He was a warrior known far and wide for his fearlessness, his cunning and, above all, his courage. The music, again, emphasized the violent exchange as explosions, crackles of electricity, and the sound of swiftly moving fireballs filled the air. The beach towels strewn along the sand where insurmountably high mountains that the super heroes needed to hurl themselves over to avoid being alternately electrocuted or burned by a super-sonic fireball. The 'transformer' became a missile launching itself with super-sonic speed toward an Island inhabited by humanoids and robots, which the people only knew as the patch of grass near the sandy beach.

The rest of the world did not exist.

And unbeknownst to the people on the sand and the people in the water, these most astonishing events were happening all around them. The people on the beach just didn't notice. They didn't notice the princesses, the horses and the super heroes. They didn't hear the music. They didn't hear the wind, the explosions or the fireballs hurtling by their very heads.

Starship

Los Angeles, California 1988

I was at a party celebrating the marriage of one of my closest friends in Los Angeles. There were 20 adults, and perhaps 2 children. A 9-year-old boy singled me out and invited me to step onto the narrow balcony just off the living room of the second story apartment building. He suggested I "hold on" as he grabbed the ebony balcony rail. I, obligingly, held on to the rail too and signaled him with a "roger" head-nod that I was ready. As he made a whooshing sound that became increasingly intense, we shot high above the apartment where all the adults were laughing and drinking below. Then, we were high above the clouds. The G force bearing down on us almost uncomfortably, the speed-of-light ascension contorted our faces as we soared into the blackness of space. Then, in a moment, we dropped back to the earth. He dusted himself off and composing himself, looked at the balcony, then he looked at me. Re-adjusting his reality to being back in an apartment with his parents, I thanked him for the ride into outer space. He, in a manner most matter of fact said, "you're welcome" and drifted back among the people in the apartment. I came back into the living room from the balcony as the dog licked moon dust off me. No one noticed the platform rocketing into outer space. And no one noticed that I'd just survived an amazing ascent on a thin balcony into the dark and starry upper atmosphere where the air was suffocatingly thin. The boy went exploring the rest of the house, probably disappearing into a closet where he was summarily beamed to a remote Venusian droid colony. I felt privileged to have been a part of his world...if only for a brief moment.

He saw that space platform so completely, that his 100% conviction made it impossible for me *not* to see what he was seeing. His invitation to the richness of his world was generous. I was allowed to experience the world inside his imagination. Now, that's magic.

These are examples of children diving directly into the infinitude of their uniquely constellated worlds: That rich, fertile soil from which all invention and creativity springs. This is the place where people are transformed and worlds are healed.

The Boy on the Balcony

Salton Sea, California April 1957

My Dad's brilliance was in knowing, intuitively, what to do when the chips were down. He unexpectedly lost his job, so we fled Los Angeles. All of us piled into our car pulling a red and white trailer that seemed to just appear on our driveway in the morning. This would give *us* a vacation and time and space for *him* to consider his next job move.

In the mid-50's, the Salton Sea was a cheap destination for Californian vacationers. In my 7-year-old innocence, I ambled up to an elderly lady that signaled me to come to where her trailer was. Seated under an awning extending from her "kitchen", she was protected from the glare of the sun off the lake. She asked me to take a seat on one of her wooden camping chairs. She looked wistfully into my eyes and spoke:

"I had a dream last night about a boy that looked just like you," she said.

"You did?" I asked.

"Yes. He was on my balcony and he was singing and singing and singing..."

She trailed off as if revisiting her dream. I sat there waiting for her to say something else as she gazed blissfully at the lake. She looked back at me and smiled. I said goodbye and walked back to our trailer. Stealing a look over my shoulder, she remained looking at me. Smiling.

The Grown Children

Vang Vieng, Laos December 2011

They looked through me. They looked past me. Young Westerners from Europe and Australia on holiday in South East Asia were very busy vacationing.

They paraded with earnest faces and backpacks down the dusty rutted streets. They disappeared down alleys and got swallowed up by store-fronts and hotels. During the day, if they weren't pulling their backpacks along, they simply were nowhere to be found.

At this point in my travels, I'd been diving in Bali and padding through Thailand for the past few months. I had seen few Westerners.

The Thai and Lao people had smiles for anyone who smiled at them. Irrespective of how they were feeling or how scarred they were from, what would have had to have been, decades of war and poverty, they always smiled when the invitation to smile presented itself. And some of these faces were as weathered and gnarled as a banyan tree trunk. This was one of the truly irresistible traits of these gentle people. No matter, the unexploded bombs in their fields and rice paddies. The wooden leg prostheses they'd made for themselves because of being in the wrong place at the wrong time as an unexploded bomb from over 40 years ago exploded on their land – kept them walking. The floods. The hundreds of years of being caught in the natural resource crossfire with their neighboring countries.

They smile. They smile when someone smiles at them.

How resilient, inspiring and brave.

And, I've watched and watched and watched. And rarely do Westerners smile at the local Lao or Thai people on the street.

~

Kayaking down the Nam Song river with two 20ish Swedish couples, each in their own kayak, the peace was unspeakable. The mountains to my right rose like prehistoric fringed humps as the river gently coaxed us downstream. The Swedes were very much in their own world. One towered over 6'. She was a stunning woman with a cream complexion whose imposing northern European beauty and stature humbled anyone shorter or less beautiful.

The Swedes were cautiously cordial with me. "What was a guy my age doing in a youthful place like this." Exactly how youthful, I was soon to discover. As we rounded a bend in the river, a wall of music assailed us like jets strafing with a deafening roar. Rickety platforms on stilts clung along the river with young people dancing a-rhythmically; lubricated with enough alcohol to make an elephant struggle to stay upright. They were everywhere. Hundreds of them. Here, in northwest Lao, it could have been Daytona Beach, Florida during Spring break.

Lao bar-staffers threw half-filled plastic bottles out to us on a long leash fully expecting to reel us in so that we could, similarly partake in the river drinking rituals at their, particular, bar-on-stilts.

It was Conrad's *Heart of Darkness* and Coppola's *Apocalypse Now* rolled into one ball of dispiriting primal madness.

These young adults were all acting happy like they do in Coke commercials. Probably the same backpacker guy that was looking past me as he intently made his way down the dusty gravel street, was now presenting his ass to river goers. Others were simply passed out or pole-dancing with imaginary poles. On one hand, I was happy for them that they were cutting loose and having fun. On the other hand, I saw them as simply slithering through the hallowed passage of adolescence into adulthood as best they knew how.

The Setting Suns

Picnic Island, Bora Bora – June 1974

I signed up for a short boat ride to one of the most photographed small Islands near Bora Bora. It was more of a thin, white sand, landing strip barely 50 yards long and maybe 14 paces wide on a good day. The water was of the ineffable turquoise sort that one only sees in exotic travel brochures: gin clear. A lone palm tree swayed against the cerulean blue of the sky.

Tropical colors dazzled the eye. As was befitting 'Picnic Island', the tour included a picnic. A picnic including a spiked coconut drink from a coconut.

While most of us swam, snorkeled and cavorted, a man in his early 70's was hunched over the straw from his coconut – his feet dug in the sand and the umbrella monkey dangling mindlessly off to one side between the strands of coconut hair. He watched the ripple on the water as he tugged at the straw with his lips. Dried sand gently fell from his calves as he probably reviewed, in dream-like succession, the events that made up his life. I caught a fleeting glimpse of his eyes: two suns setting in a hazy sky. His smile said, "It doesn't get better than this. I've arrived." His heart said, "All that, for this moment? Is that it?"

What happened? What happens between the sand castles on the beach and the pole-dancing alongside the river? What happens between the first day on the job and the moment we're on vacation, in retirement, watching our toes wriggling in the sand through the haze of a coco-loco?

What happened to *me*?

This is what I'd guess happened:

Part One

The Loss of Innocence

CHAPTER 1

The Sound

I imagine the following:

Waves were lapping on a distant shore. Galaxies whirled powered by a low hum as if someone was intoning the sound of all life. The sound vibrated within everything. It was constant and it created life. Within this cascading and unstoppable orgasm of sound vibration, pulsation and vibrant color, there was something that so purely spoke of home. A home that had no beginning, middle or end.

Its vibration enriched the very fabric of this profound and abiding sense of belonging. And as the sound increased its vibration and urgency, another universe created itself. With tingling divisions happening at a velocity of near frenzy, the sound organized randomness into order. I watched as my body assembled itself. I watched like a lover watches the sunset. I watched with amazement. This body had a purpose, and its purpose was to create itself. And like a city being erected from the ground up in fast motion, the cells carried out their duties with an inexorable and insect-like precision. The conductor was the sound itself. The orchestra was the body: A beautiful symphony of creation crescendoing to a near deafening pitch. And at the crest of that musical mountain of sound, I fused my awareness with this body...as it kicked and twitched into life.

She, now, presided over this continental aural landscape giving constant assurance of safety, survival and comfort. The many textures of undulating sound pulsed like the ancient memory of waves alternately lapping and crashing in my consciousness. And underlying the whooshing of fluid everywhere was a drumming coming from her. Constant and assuring, the drum beat was a deep and sonorous thumping that shook, at times, like the thunder from a dark tropical Isle followed by a gentle rain. And, like the sun, it was warming. Constellations of sensation and prismatic color heaved and swirled. The sound was alive with creation. And the creation was alive with sound.

Gently rocking on an ocean of warmth, there existed the profoundest comfort. And sensing the sweet dulcet tones of a faraway song as she spoke, a profoundly deep relaxation stilled this awareness of mine until it was like a deep and clear pool. The melodic incantations from her voice lulled me into a state of profound relaxation even though this tiny and still formless body was creating itself at break-neck speed as tiny organs sprung to life and my little heart pulsed in sympathetic rhythm to hers.

Not only food, but an undeniable sense of belonging was issued into the center of my body. The tones from her musical voice reverberated with ancestral memories. Memories of all the mothers of her lineage. The soft rise and fall of her voice vibrated my being with the mental impressions of all time and of all life, everywhere. Feeling her voice folding around me was like being witness to the song of all the mothers of the universe singing to each other the song of love.

Singing each other into existence.

The song of life itself.

And all time ran together in the water world. And though the tidal moods of the ocean changed like the phases of the moon, the ocean was always there gently rocking. The ocean whispered eternity and never was there doubt about my belonging...not for a second of this wondrous, kaleidoscopic time spent being one in the primordial comfort her water world sanctum. My thoughts were her thoughts. Her thoughts were my thoughts. I lived for her. And she lived for me. We were one. I floated and basked in this supernal and exquisite warmth of her ocean. In the warmth of the womb, I was in the cradle of all life. My being was in the belly of all there was. There was nothing else. This ephemeral water world was my home as well as the deep drone of the sound that created me.

The End of the Sound

Like a soft dark cloud, this body of mine went numb just as the sound became unsettling. The colors that made my home comfortable and warm became angry and unfamiliar. The eternity of my ocean womb came to an abrupt and violent dead end. There came to be a flurry of unfamiliar sounds. Violent quakes. The gentle lapping of waves were now crashing violently. And where these billowy walls once enfolded me gently like a cloud, they became a menacing and impersonal enclosure now intent on expelling me from the soothing comfort of the sound. I tried to oblige the spasmodic urgings of the walls around me, but my body wasn't responding. My body was suddenly limp and unresponsive. The sublime muffled tones of my mother, were now sharp. A cacophony of other voices frightened me. My world was changing. The world was changing.

A blinding light.

~

There was the sound of panic and shrill crying somewhere outside in a distant universe. I was assailed by loud aggressive noises that felt brittle, metallic and unsettling. This body of mine twisted, heaved and fought. My limbs rigidified and flared. Racing to make sense of this new galaxy of cold colors and shrill sounds, the warm and watery embrace had now become a world of seeming infinite cold space.

Chilled, unfamiliar and more than anything...separated from her and absolutely terrified, I needed to know where she was. Where her presence could formerly only be felt, there was no feeling her. No hearing her. The far away voice was replaced by loud noises that quaked my body. Loud noises that felt unsafe. Loud noises that shattered these tender ears.

My eyes serving up nothing more than blurry holograms of a new universe, I looked for her everywhere. I looked but couldn't see. I looked frantically, but couldn't see.

Bereft and alone like an astronaut, I dangled in space. Precarious and utterly alone.

Then.

There she was – an angel amidst the chaos and commotion of strident voices, clanging metal instruments and frantically moving rubber hands. Something allowed this one single apparition to pierce the blurry veil. And though she was barely visible, she was younger and more beautiful than could have ever been imagined. Tendrils of wet hair clung to her face, like Amphitrite coming up for air after a sumptuous swim in her warm Neptune's sea. There she was. The quest complete. Together again. We were complete. Our eyes locked and we gazed at each other with what seemed to be a rapturous eternity. We were in love. It would be alright, but if only I could have touched that soft, warm skin.

My lifeline to her was severed. I panicked. And, something else was terribly wrong:

A sudden, and unexpectedly urgent, breath of air came pushing into my lungs as they inflated like a billowed sail.

My little chest seared with the antiseptic dryness of this new and foreign gas – air. This enemy, air, came flooding between me and her. I was now cold, separate and powerless. The distant far off and frighteningly shrill cries kept speeding closer toward me with the inexorability of a speeding night train. I was terrified. Amphitrite was terrified.

These people I'd never heard before handled me with an abruptness that was foreign to my ocean world. I was poked and prodded by cold, unfeeling hands. Measured and weighed, all I wanted was my mother's skin. Cold metal was shoved against my chest. Swabs were forced up my nostrils and both of my eyes were crisply daubed with something that stung like the dickens. A bright light felt like it was boring a hole into my eyes. My body was on fire and cold at the same time and no one was there to let me know I'd be alright. No one.

My perfect universe was gone in an instant. The perfectly sustaining universe providing food, protection and clean-up. Gone. And the world, as I knew it, was forever changed.

Where we were once one, we were now two and the initiation into two-ness felt foreign and rude.

The sharp sound of crying, that started out so far away, now rang in my ears. And the crying was now, suddenly, coming from me. I just wanted the assurance of knowing I was safe. The feeling of skin and not the cold, impersonal and lifeless touch of linen, metal or wood.

I needed her desperately.

She seemed spent, bewildered and distant.

I was separated from her. My chest burned and ached. No one seemed to hear. No one seemed the least bit concerned. I had just stepped into hell and there was no apparent way back from where I'd come.

An eternity of tensing my muscles and crying for help gave way to a fitful, albeit merciful, sleep and just when things couldn't have gotten worse, a searing pain shot to my brain from my groin as my skin was dispassionately cut off by the rubber-gloved guys. What WAS this place?! I'd gone from such comfort into a world characterized by such unfeeling savagery in a matter of minutes. Who were these guys, anyway?! This was planet hell. And this was my welcome.

All I wanted was to be held and never put down.

All I wanted was to be held.

Me and my Dad - Hollywood, California - 1950

CHAPTER 2

Ooom

THE CRYING GAVE way, ultimately, to exhaustion. And exhaustion became the sweet precursor to sleep. Sleep: Where the dreams would shuttle me back to the former rightness of a world knitted in muffled and assuring velvety tones that fell on my ears with the sound of all that was caring, soft and warm.

I often was alone and helpless. Unsafe on an inhospitable planet, it was so very unlike the warm interior galaxy of my former home. When I was touched, it was altogether too abbreviated. It was all together not enough. So I contented myself with not enough. This was the deal on the air planet. But, I didn't rule out crying all together. There was still the vague hope that someone would notice – if I cried long and hard enough. And someone always did notice.

The diversions from my burning requirement for contact seemed plentiful enough. The lights flickering as prismatic out-of-focus amorphous shapes danced around everywhere. They swelled and receded in this new and endless universe. Parading, dancing and streaking in front of these eyes, these blurry forms were also part of this new and exotic surround. The color floated above, sometimes slowly. Sometimes quickly. But, there was the ever-presence of round watery color. A soft shadow from which low tones emanated, and another from which high tones floated and swam all around my body. Coalescing to make a symphony of sensation, this rapidly-becoming-familiar world was completely different from the water planet.

Body sensations were leaping up the spine. But what were these limbs and toes and fingers? What an amazing and delightful notion! They moved on their own. Then, they moved because something deep in my chest asked them to move. Then this body became an instrument of sense perception, movement and sound as the whole of the machinery sprang to life. The body machine was wondrous and fascinating. How the muscles tightened! How the legs twitched! How the mouth sputtered! How noises and fricatives lurched from this mouth of mine. There was no end to the discoveries announcing themselves in every moment. Every moment paraded endless discovery.

The toes glistened under the light overhead. They flared and danced. There were so many of them all moving about as if they each had little minds of their own. Little pink things wriggling this way and that. If I could have gotten them into my mouth, I would have. They had to be as interesting in my mouth as they were to look at.

The sweet and exotic fragrances of "Balloon" and baby talc.

The endless wonder of the balloon's smoothness.

The way the light played on the balloon.

The balloon was such a happy and whimsical planet basking in the warmth of its sun. The hypnotic scent of "balloon" sent this mind reeling with the promise of the multitudinous discoveries on the wonder-horizon. "Balloon" even made a noise as my body tumbled against it. A noise that first startled, then amused with an indescribable delight. "Balloon" moved all around me of its own accord, playing and even sticking to my body. "Balloon" was the first playmate. Cavorting. Reflecting kaleidoscopic light and always squeaking, "Balloon" had taste and a feel and a smell. And the colors radiating from "Balloon" were like the colors in the water world. They were bright, rich and familiar. They were wondrous. They were becoming part of a new home. Until.

POP!

And it was all gone in the wink of an eye. The limp and shriveled remains lay helplessly in my crib.

The sensations, though, continued like an ever revolving carousel. The sheer joy of scents everywhere.

My world kick-started with my mother's every visit to my wood-barred and linen home. Oh good, I'm going to live!

And then, as she mysteriously left my crib-side:

Oh shit, I'm going to die.

Coming from the primordial blood and briny warmth of the most perfect of embraces into a startling and altogether strange new world was an adventure. Daytime was a discovery punctuated with fleeting moments of bliss. A bliss plumped up with wonder and a gurgling delight. A brain abuzz with new information. The sensations of hunger, fullness, fatigue and the profoundly frustrating lack of facility to make the discomforts known. It was new. Every inch of this terrain. Every sound, smell, color and sensation. Every jostle, every poke, every diaper change. Though strangely familiar for these virgin senses, every bit of information coming into this brain was new. And the newness was thrilling.

All new. All the time.

No need to consider the brutality of my entry into the air planet. There were too many *distractions*. There were too many wondrous distractions.

The Night

At night, with little contact from mother or father and light years away from the warm familiar sanctum of the world before, I cried. I cried because I was frightened and feeling unsafe in the profoundest and most ancient and visceral of ways. The night transformed all the familiar objects in my room into eery representations of themselves. The playful colors of day had retreated and I was left to make sense of this darkness alone. In the darkness, my indefatigable crying would inevitably give way to the daylight when the miraculous world of colored plastic balls and a mobile of toy birds swaying idly over my crib amused me endlessly. And the most cherished of all moments...just being held.

Months later, which seemed like an eternity of dizzyingly voluminous data input, another discovery was made: "Ooom". These huge brown eyes of mine beheld the "Ooom".

Unlike "Balloon", the presence of the "Ooom" held me transfixed as I'd intone a long and thoughtful, "Ooom" as I regarded this luminous, white balloon outside the night window: The miracle of the "Ooom".

Moonstruck, my attention was fixed on this unearthly orb. My eyes widened whenever the moon's familiar, pale light bathed the small, square room that came to be the new universe. It was a friend. Because of this new friend, I cried less at night, because I knew it would be looking in on me sooner or later. Familiar and mystical, it was the guardian that lovingly watched over me. The shimmering sphere, hung in the blackness of a starry sky, warmed the insides of a boy barely a few months old. That fateful day of expulsion from my sanctum, now seemed like a distant and alien star. Held in the safety of the "Ooom's" glow, we regarded each other with solemnity and recognition. And, with an undeniable respect.

"Ooom".

An earnest attempt was made to steady this wobbling head as I found myself awash in the cool blue reflected light of the moon and, ceremonially, all light and shadow danced for this magical new friend. More reliable than "Balloon", "Ooom never surprised me with an explosive 'pop' even though it did hide away for nights at a time. Finally falling asleep as I lay strangely alone in this altogether foreign land of ghoulishly undulating shapes, the comforting sense of the "Ooom" was all around me. The "Ooom" knew the sound from which I came. The "Ooom" knew about the water world. The "Ooom" knew about my mother's song. The "Ooom" knew.

The "Ooom" shed soft pools of light as they changed their shape on the wood floor of my bedroom and on the walls. Melting together, the light's phantasm enveloped the room as well as the little body within it. Sweetly urging me to sleep. And sleep I did as all the soldiers of cell, bone and tissue growth dutifully went about their business...all under the watchful eye of the luminescent and magical moon.

The Backyard

The sun outside shed a dazzling light on everything in my portable crib. The leaves in the trees shimmered and danced in the warm glow of the sun. Everything loved the sun:

The clouds.

The blue.

And the birds in the trees.

The sun was worth chatting about. And the birds seemed to have so much to say about it. Under the soft shade of the trees, I observed a completely new world as the birds made these curiously urgent sounds. Left there for hours, I'd watch the birds as they'd endlessly busy themselves with feeding, conversing and flitting from one tree branch to another. What a wonderfully social world this was! Wings would beat and flutter as these busy creatures of the air would staccato from branch to branch and tree to tree. And my eyes were fixed on them. Trying always to keep up with their rapid movements and musical chatter. Again, the brain was racing to keep up with an unrelenting flood of information. Life-on-the-wing dancing in the air producing a foreign sound never before heard. The tone of the bird song fell on my ears like a million melodies singing together. Concertizing together. The world of the birds swelled in intensity as every bird had something extremely important to say. They spoke in imperatives. It was emphatic. Inexplicably, the birds would sometimes go dead quiet as if someone said something that stopped them all in their tracks. I looked around for the reason they'd all gone quiet when little by little they would start up again louder and more necessitous than before. The world of birds was an always different and always exciting community of song and lightning fast movement. I would watch the birds for hours. I never tired of their music, their movements or their flight. Never for a moment.

There was also magic in the dirt and in the infinitude of life parading about within it. The sow bugs, worms and ants were all part of this elaborate earthen tapestry. Weaving, tumbling insects of the ground always purposeful as they clumsily made their ways on the surface of the soil. Then, these creatures would inevitably disappear into the dark rich loam. I was lost in the smell of the earth. All life and death was contained within the rich smell of the soil. Older than old and thick with thousands of teaming microscopic life-forms, it seemed that all life arose from within the moist folds of the earth. Golden sparkles within the dirt, caught the sun's light and flashed across my eyes. The dark ground was teaming with every kind of life imaginable as it pulsed and heaved before my eyes – a living, undulating thing.

Always new.

Always a wonder.

Always a discovery.

My Brother

Many "Oooms" later, my brother was born. A tiny muscular baby fidgeting and twisting like a worm on a hook, he was wedged on the floor between the front and back seat of our Hudson. One year old, I looked at my newly born and wrinkled baby brother. I gave him a silent nod of welcome. His eyes trained on mine as he tried steadying his head that was new to the sensation of gravity exerting itself on him. He was unsure and suspicious of his new environment. After acknowledging me, he returned to being a newborn, as if he'd momentarily forgotten where he was, and continued his wriggling.

What had previously been a universe of dazzling lights and exotic sounds began to fade as my mother's responsibilities started tugging at her. The duties of being a wife and mother had started fraying every corner of her world.

The daily visits to the world of the birds and the world of the soil were more frequent as she'd park me there knowing that I'd be entertained, and quiet, for hours on end so she could care for my brother. The firmament on which all my joys and discoveries were made, formerly unquestioned, was now shifting. I was profoundly dependent on my parents. And they were stretched. A world *without* the continual assurance of mother and father was a frightening one. One too frightening to even fathom.

My parents, in spite of everything, raised two boys and a girl. And I was often amazed at just how well they managed to do it. I admired, even as a young boy, how great a team they made and I hoped that one day I'd be in a relationship like that..

As for the "Ooom", it's importance began to fade.

The sense that something was 'not quite right' seated itself squarely in my belly.   Whether that was simply something I came in with, I'll never know. But it persisted for a long time.

CHAPTER 3

The Winds of Change

T HERE WAS NOT enough of my mother to go around. My father worried about not having a wife that was emotionally and physically there for him because my mother was starting to show signs of wear under the demands of motherhood. The more he was stressed at work, the more he needed her consolation. The more she was pressured by the constant requirements of two small boys, the more she needed his help. The poles of the circus tent faltered then toppled over as the tent wilted slowly to the ground. The circus had come and gone.

My brother and I were harbors for each other as we tried making emotional sense of the new normal which had become: *fragile*. The tension in my body echoed a continuing sense that something wasn't right. So, a shift happened. A shift away from all things wondrous, to all things tenuous.

But in spite of the shift away from being the center of my parents' world, there were distractions. And, the distractions were interesting. And, there were many of them.

Shiny Things

The box of buttons in our hall closet held a fascination for me. They were button samples that my father would sell as a textile representative. When freed from the dark lifelessness of the hall closet, the buttons came to life as variously opalescent or abalone-like gems. Other buttons were multifaceted and colorful reflecting light in ways that hypnotized me -- reminiscent of a distant star. And I stared at them. Sometimes for hours. I felt that there was an answer in the color. Color was fascinating. Color was mystical.

The song of the birds was replaced by the songs coming from a small red radio in the kitchen.

Music.

I would retreat into the music. Inside the music was a familiarity and a calm that reminded me of life inside the belly. And my world started to knit itself together with a musical needle. The sound of the wind; the song of the birds; the imperceptible noises from the earth all seemed to be contained in the wondrous sounds emanating from the little red radio in the kitchen. With a sublime and enchanting entreaty, the music reawakened in me a sense of rightness. The music held within it something enchanting and familiar.

Classical music, in particular, spoke to me. Though the fidelity out of the red kitchen radio must have left something to be desired, my imagination coaxed color and excitement out of it. The warmth of the strings, especially the cello, suggested the sound of the human voice. The French horns heralded the coming of the dawn. The oboes suggested whimsy and, at times, a sorrow too great to bear. I saw landscapes. Running horses. Mountains. Flowers. Lakes. Of all the things in my life at the time, music evoked the richest pallet for my imagination. And every bird song and sound of the earth and sky now lived inside me.

Of Hot Water and Hallucinations

When I was four, the boiling water that scalded my legs was like a stop sign in the middle of the road. My life changed in that instant. The pain had me in the unyielding grip of an eagle's claw as the searing burn scorched any hope for relief. The morphine-induced haze skewed all sense of time and place. When my parents came to visit me in the 1950's intensive care unit, they seemed like dreamy reminders of the parents I had. In and out of wakefulness, the often freakish world around me seemed an eerie and wholly unfriendly place. Splayed naked and vulnerable on a hospital bed for an interminable 8 days, I remember only discomfort, poking, prodding and an endless stream of strangers. This cold and antiseptic world was re-mindful, in the most unsettling of ways, of the time spent in the hospital at birth. Separated from my parents and in the company of the ghastly drug induced phantasms, I stared at the hospital room door waiting for my parents to burst into the room to make it all go away.

For many years afterward, I was haunted by dreams trying to communicate with my parents. In the dream, I'd see them and try to speak and they couldn't hear me. And when they *did* hear me, they'd hear me several minutes, often several days, later. Their response, similarly, took several days to reach me. It was like I was on one side of the earth and they were on the other and there was this vexing and frightening time-lag in our communication.

My father would sit beside my hospital bed as I searched my father's face for an answer.

"What happened? I don't know what happened, do you?"

And in my morphine-addled reality, he swam into my field of vision and floated out just as unexpectedly.

Once home, morphine's residual affective surrealism exerted itself on this small body elasticizing an already stretched imagination to its very borders. The faded sense of wonder was replaced by often macabre images of shadows dancing on the wall. Strange sounds crept into my room from the outside at night. I'd need to look under my bed to make sure nothing was under there, but the still searing pain on my legs made it too difficult to do even that. The world was unsafe. The environment was ever-shifting. The people were foreign. The music playing in my head was the only safe place. The only place I wanted to be.

In my room, I lay under a lighted canopy for several months. Something in the canopy's light was to have made the healing of my legs happen more quickly. The bright lights made sleeping fitful, though. Still naked, helpless and on fire, isolation and discomfort became familiar. And music was the only thing that chased away the nagging suspicion that I'd never be right again.

Music was the abiding, the secret and forever friend. I framed every experience; every feeling within a musical context. The music danced uncontrollably in my head. Some melodies I'd heard before while others would simply bubble up from somewhere inside me.

A year later, while lying in bed, the grief welled up in my chest of all that I'd lost. I'd lost a body that was comfortable. I'd lost my wondrous "Ooom". Every loss and every emotion in my life was somehow mirrored by a song that described that emotion better than I could ever articulate. The songs played in my head obsessively and instead of going to sleep that night, I cried. And I couldn't stop. I tried to stop, but couldn't manage it. My brother, in the bunk below me asked,

"Why are you crying?"

"I don't know," I said.

"You should stop," he reminded me.

"I know, but I can't."

My father, dutifully, came into our bedroom and hit me until I stopped. I knew he really didn't want to hit me, but he felt duty bound to restore peace to the house, I guess. Besides, that's what parents did back then to make sure a child didn't get too spoiled. If a parent came to the child every time he was crying, that child was destined to be a sissy – and, a spoiled and irascible one at that.

Me - age 4

CHAPTER 4

You're not going to leave me here...

I WAS FOUR. My mother took me to a group of cold-rectangular buildings. We walked inside one of them. A smell permeated the air that suggested cut trees, chalk dust and a floor cleanser. There were other mothers with their children as well. Weary, my mother put on her bravest face.

"This is where you'll probably do finger-painting," she said, pointing with her chin toward one of the desks in a long row of desks. We walked up to one of the desks mid-row and in the middle of the classroom.

She pressed her hand against the freshly varnished pine desk. Removing her hand, the soft imprint of her fingers lingered then evaporated before my eyes. Instinctively, I felt something sinister was about to happen. Dazed, I furtively stole glances at the other children with their parents. All of them were happy. It was a new adventure for every one of them. But what kind of adventure was this for me? Not a backyard adventure. Not a rich, deep soil adventure. Not a neighborhood adventure. I was certain this was going to be another experience like in the hospital, but it was only being packaged differently.

"And, this lady over here will be your teacher," my mother continued as she walked along the chalkboard skipping her index finger over one of the grooves in the aluminum chalk tray. Walking up to Miss Corey, my mother turned around to me and took my hand. I clutched her hand tightly.

"Michael, this is your teacher, Miss Corey," my mother offered with the utmost social grace.

I looked down. Miss Corey leaned down to me with a sweet smile and big, welcoming brown eyes.

"Hello, Michael," she said with a soft mother's voice. I stole a glance at her.

The following day my mother drove me to "kindergarten". She walked me to room number 7. This was the same featureless bungalow and nondescript wooden door that we'd walked through the day before. This is where I met Miss Corey and saw all the other children with their parents. We walked in and my mother assured me that I would have fun here. I looked at her wordlessly, my eyes begging that she not leave. But she did. I couldn't understand why she would leave me behind with people I had never seen before: people I didn't know. A torrent of emotion swept over me not knowing if I was most shaky about being abandoned or whether I was worried that there would be no one to take care of her with me in "kindergarten". The classroom door closed with a sickening *kuh-clunk* as my eyes shot between the children obediently sitting on the floor and the starkness of the un-feeling door that separated me from my mother whose steps reverberated down the cement walkway as she made her way to the car.

Bereft, I drifted to the desk that probably still had my mother's scent from the day before. It probably still had some part of her lingering there. I'd settle for anything: a fingerprint, a thread from her sweater...anything.

"..you'll probably do finger-painting here..." her sweet voice whispered in my ears. I wanted her to be there in the room with me. This was an alien and cold place, like the hospital, with strange and unknown people and smells. Home was familiar. And this place was both far from home and little-known to me. All I could think of was running after her. I fought the urge. I fought it with all my might. Would she even come back and pick me up? I couldn't remember her saying anything about coming back to pick me up. I panicked and as I settled, numb and disbelieving into the wooden chair beside the 'finger-painting' desk, I sunk my head between my folded arms at the very spot my mother's hand had touched. I attempted to stifle my crying but the tears made their way down my cheeks anyway. And as each tear slid off my nose, they dripped and washed away the very spot where my mother's fingerprint had come and gone merely 24 hours before.

Lost in this foreign land, with unfamiliar faces, the tears kept coming. It had only been a few months since the nightmarish experience in the hospital and a whole summer of lying beneath the heat canopy to heal my burnt arms and legs. And now, this. More strangers. I still needed to be cared for. My legs weren't even healed. They ached. The wildest thoughts swam around my head. I was going to die. I knew it.

As if from heaven, music wafted from near the chalkboard to where I was sitting:

"Would you like to come join us?" cooed Miss Corey. I peered up from my wet arms to see, maybe, 20 children seated on a rug in front of Miss Corey as she looked sweetly at me. I scanned the other tables. I was the only child not seated on the floor in front of our teacher. The other children looked at me patiently, also nervous at the new surroundings.

Wiping my face of the tears, I ambled cautiously over to the others and found a little patch of variegated rug where a girl had scooted to one side making room for me. I sat next to her 'Indian-Style'. She looked at me and smiled sweetly, and then obediently looked back to Miss Corey.

The endlessly compassionate lilt of Miss Corey's voice softened the otherwise jarring experience. She spoke in dulcet, measured sentences. I was instantly calmed by the sweet melodic strains of her voice. The girl next to me stole a look at me and smiled. She looked backed at Miss Corey and probably thought to herself:

"Yeah. He'll be ok."

I was in love with my teacher and the girl seated next to me. I'd barely been away from home for an hour, and already...I was in love.

Dolcedo, Italy - 2011

CHAPTER 5

Recurring Dreams

RECURRING DREAM #1

I PUSHED A BABY carriage around the neighborhood where we lived: A sprawling tract of box-like homes offered to post World War II servicemen through the GI bill, they spread like Legos across the San Fernando Valley to quickly accommodate a population spurt that Los Angeles enjoyed in the half decade after V Day. Bordered by alfalfa fields and farms, these tracts denuded of trees and bushes, came to be known as Reseda, Tarzana, Van Nuys and Encino. It was the mid-50's, and I was 5 years old. In the dream, I wheeled the carriage from house to house collecting babies. I was in love with these babies. Innocent, I wanted them all to myself. I wanted to protect them. I knew I could make them safe. I wanted to save them all from their parents. It was my duty to protect each one.

I tenderly placed each baby into the baby carriage until the soft, velvety carriage lining was filled to capacity. My heart, too, was filled to capacity. Filled with love for each one of them, I looked deeply into their eyes and they in mine. Each baby was a jewel. Every one was different and special.

--

This was the most compelling sense of rightness I'd ever had before. This was the strongest sense of rightness I've ever known since.

RECURRING DREAM #2

Like in an Escher painting, babies were on endless conveyor belts. Stark, gray and metallic gears rolled tirelessly. Each factory baby was wrapped in swaddling. All of them were destined for some place and some family unknown. Each of them the same, there was an eery lack of spirit to them all. Noiselessly and without protest, they lay on an assembly line.

I was four or five and watched, helpless, from a metal platform perch in the dream. I thought to myself, as I watched, that babies weren't nurtured for their uniqueness, rather they were stamped out like products manufactured for some larger purpose.

CHAPTER 6

Elementary School

MISS COREY HAD become a memory. I ached for the soft and welcoming brown eyes I seemed to be able to walk into. Other women I'd see in the super market looked like her from behind. My heart would stop. I'd run to catch up and it was never her. It was never the woman that could soothe my nerves with just the soft music of her voice. Kindergarten was a dream replaced by elementary school. Kindergarten was the teaser. Elementary school was my introduction to the militaristic hand of discipline.

Amazingly, I had the prescience to suspect that I'd have to give up a part of myself to fit into school. It simply wasn't in my nature to take and obey orders unquestioningly. The punishment of staying 'after school' for falling out of line was simply too harrowing a prospect, so I did what was asked of me. Reluctantly, I obeyed my teachers knowing full well that I was about to hold my breath for 12 years until, at some point, I could try to reclaim myself.

In school I was constantly accused of being a daydreamer. Daydreaming was anti-social. Daydreaming was condemned. It didn't fit into school. The daydreaming wasn't appreciated at home either.

"Stop your daydreaming. Wake up. Wake up. You're not going to get anywhere if you're off in the clouds somewhere."

Looking out of the window seemed the only natural thing to do. It was easy. It was like breathing. It was where I wanted to be. Outside. The birds awaited me. The clouds were soft, white and ever-changing. There were things to discover. Things on the upper limbs of trees. Things in the air. Things in the ground. The air was clean out there. None of this cafeteria, chalk, disinfectant or milk carton smell. I wanted out. On the magical days when I faked being ill or having a stomach ache and was outside of school's jurisdiction, I reveled in that limitless world of the imagination outside of the school walls.

The world on the seams of where I was supposed to be and what I was supposed to be doing.

The culture was swift at trying to imprint its codes on me:

Follow the rules.

And the rules pressed in from all sides. There were rules about conduct on the playground. There were rules about how to behave in the classroom. There were rules about being "on time". The rules and the clock on the wall, after all, were partners in this conveyor-belt world. And they had to be obeyed. And the adult that purveyed those rules watched over us with a ruler tapping impatiently in an opened hand. Without rules, there was no order. Without rules, nothing could get done. If I didn't obey those rules, life could get downright unfriendly.

School quite simply was the nightmare of the hospital continued.

Miss Sunstead made me long for the gentleness of Miss Corey with such a pang that I spent very much of the 3rd grade in the nurse's office. Miss Sunstead's metallic New York accent and strident vocal cadences kept me on edge and kept my stomach acid production in full swing. To have her look at me with that glare was as unsettling as unsettling got. I had stomach aches that were my excuse to not be in her class. The truly banner days won me a trip back home. And I just did not understand why my mother insisted I go back to school the following day. I felt so fundamentally betrayed. And ironically, on some level I knew my mother was doing what was expected of her. She knew her kids had to be in school and she made sure we were. Underneath the disciplinary actions of my mother and father, I always felt that I was loved. I knew that at the bottom of their abiding love for me, they were conflicted at having to be the parent and the disciplinarian because sometimes those roles were at variance with how they actually felt. They would have just as soon gone on family picnics and lie under the shade of a tree watching the clouds drifting idly by. And I would have loved that. I often thought of proposing to them:

> "Could we just forget about this whole public school thing and enjoy life? Go on camping trips. Travel a little. I know Dad's gotta work, but I'd be happy to pitch in. We could work as a family somewhere. At least we could be together and not have Dad going off to work and me and Dan going off to school. We could be a team. Yeah. A team."

Dinosaurs

Kellogg's corn flakes had a special on dinosaur figurines. Sending a box-top or two to an address in Battle Creek, Michigan would result in getting a two inch long molded plastic dinosaur a month later. "Collect all 12!" the cereal box would announce. I would eagerly await the arrival of each new dinosaur in the coveted small cardboard box from Battle Creek, Michigan. They were my friends. I even took my favorite, probably a plesiosaur, to school with me. Tucked safely in my pocket, it was something familiar. Something friendly. Out on the playground, during recess after lunch one autumn day, I imagined my plesiosaur to be flying through the air with its aquatic wings and long neck. Holding it up close to my eyes as it was winging its way around a remote corner of the playground, the playground monitor plucked it right out of my hands and looked at me scornfully like I'd committed some egregious crime.

"Come to my classroom after school, and I'll give it back to you. You have no business having a toy at school," she reprimanded. "Come to bungalow 9."

"Bungalow 9?!. Bungalow 9?!?!?," I thought. That was where all the sixth graders were. Since I was a second grader and we were finished with school at 2pm, the sixth graders would all be in class until 3pm, and I'd be shamed and ridiculed in front of the older kids. There was no pain greater than the shame of being made to look childish in front of the older kids. When school finished, I walked to Bungalow 9 and stared at the steps leading to the door.

Like a military bungalow and separate from the rest of the school buildings, it loomed stark and imposing as the heat rose off the asphalt in the early afternoon sun. Would I wait until after 3pm or be brave and claim my plesiosaurus in front of the critical eyes of the big kids? I must have stared at the door for 20 minutes before swallowing hard to gingerly make my way up the wooden stairs to knock feebly at the door.

"Yes?" came the reply on the other side of the door that caused my shoulders to creep up the side of my neck. I meekly opened the door to see 30 6th graders scrutinizing me because I was small, weak and apologetic looking. The other kids loved pouncing on the weak and pitiful.

The teacher, without skipping a beat or so much as acknowledging me, stopped her lecture and dipped into her upper left-hand desk drawer producing my plastic dinosaur from Battle Creek, Michigan for all the class to see. My heart stopped. I wanted to snatch my dinosaur from her spindly fingers and sprint home.

"It makes you wonder, sometimes, why anyone would ever want to play with a toy like this," she said looking thoughtfully at the flying dinosaur. "Maybe you have to be young or in a dream world to enjoy a plastic toy..." She drifted away, momentarily as if longing for a time, long buried, when this was ex*actly* something that she would do. Catching herself in her reverie, she walked over to me, looking to her 6th grade audience hoping that they were appreciating the example that was being made of me. She handed over the small green toy dinosaur. Not looking up at her or at the sixth graders who were now snickering about the childish second-grader standing apologetically before them, I turned tail and made my way out the door and started on the 45 minute-long walk home – re-united, finally, with my dinosaur friend knowing that he could help take the shame away. I solemnly vowed to keep my dreams and plastic friends to myself.

The Private World

If it hadn't been for the traumatic episode with my burned legs and the confounding restrictiveness that was public school, I might have never created the private dream world: The secret garden where no one else was allowed. It was something I could call my own and that dream world was softly nestled into a nest lined with musical strains: A musical tapestry made up of loud, soft, brave, sweet, daring, commanding or comforting orchestrations. Simply: music became the ally and friend in an increasingly unfamiliar, and often hostile, world. The music that poured out of the little red radio in the kitchen kept me tethered…kept my imagination alive. And what a very strange concept: A radio – playing music. Where was it coming from? And how did the music arrive in in these radio contraptions? It was magic and the whole concept of radio waves held endless fascination for me.

One Christmas, I got a small battery-powered lantern. One bulb shone a soft white light, and when I selected the other bulb with a crude metal toggle, it signaled a red S.O.S. I knew that one day, we'd be camping and my little lantern would come in handy to light the way. And if we were ever in trouble, the feebly blinking red light would signal to our rescuers that we needed help. In the meantime, though, I contented myself to watch as the red flashing light signaled distress. I watched it tirelessly under the covers of my bed. Sometimes, I put it on the window sill wondering if anyone would notice. Anyone at all. The lantern was the barometer for happy and sad. When I was happy, the white light shone peacefully in my room casting a shadow of the lantern's base that housed the two batteries that I always hoped would last longer than they did. I would swing the lantern as the shadows around the room danced from the many angles of the its white light.

At around the same time, I got a transistor radio and it set me free to listen to whatever music I wanted. The red kitchen radio played merrily during the day, while my small transistor radio was safely and secretly tucked under my pillow as I'd listen to its muffled music that would transport me before going to sleep. Long after my parents had announced a 'lights out and music off' for the evening, I listened late into the night until hearing the song that would complete the day for me and send me tumbling off into a deep sleep. It was an altogether secret world of music and the light of a lantern.

Music contained all my emotions and it expressed them so much better than I ever could have. It described places in the world I hadn't seen. And, somehow, where nothing or no one else understood, music did. Music always understood: It understood the struggle of life announcing itself in the face of the ever-present danger:

The Rules.

There were, however, those adults that noticed and respected that private place. They understood the private place because they probably had their own private place. Miss Corey understood the private place. At the very least, she respected it. Much later, I found out that she was an alcoholic. Frankly, that didn't diminish this Goddess one little bit in my estimation. She understood the madness, the pain, and the lack of caring around her. Even though she couldn't have been more than 25 years old, she knew about the struggle. That's what made her so utterly accessible and so sweetly warmhearted. The softness in her voice said it all. She understood about the struggle, the madness, and life's sharp edges. But like for many of us, she reached for something, in her case – alcohol, that could help her through the toughest times.

And there were those that wielded discipline like it was their right as a grownup.

-Stay within the rules and you're a good person.

-Ignore the rules and you're a renegade and your behavior is punishable by ostracism.

Sure, discipline kept me safe. I knew how to keep myself safe from running out in front of a car but it inadvertently crushed something vital. It suppressed an innocence and creativity that was desperate to express itself. That desperation to express myself actually got me in trouble.

CHAPTER 7

Iris

S WEPT UP IN the kind of passion that only a fifth grader can muster, I extemporized in front of my class about the richness contained in the music of Johannes Brahms, while all the other kids gave their music reports on Bill Haley, Buddy Holly and the most exciting of newcomers: Elvis.

For me, the music of Brahms took me to the softest of places. It washed over me. It sang to me from within my chest. Brahms knew something I wanted to know. Something I wanted to experience. His music clung to the corners of our modest living room long after our new HiFi was shut off. The notes nestled into the drapes at the living room window. The lingering musical strains awaited being brought back to life again the next time I'd turn on the HiFi to listen and be transported on yet another musical adventure. Brahms knew me and Brahms understood. He understood about the suffocating world of "Rules". He knew of the world of birds. He knew about the moon. He most certainly knew about the private world that needed to be kept private and he knew about the likes of Iris Stevens.

I was in love with Iris Stevens.

The skip in her step beneath her ankle-length dress.

The pony tail dancing on her shoulders as she flew around the auditorium that doubled as a dance space.

The constellation of freckles on her quick-to-smile face.

Her southern accent.

Her switched on energy.

I loved Iris. And she liked me. The gentle squeeze she gave my hand assured me of her attraction to me when we ended up dancing together during our sixth grade square dance hour. Once, next to the white picket fence that gayly traced the perimeter of her house, I declared my support of Richard Nixon in his campaign for president. Even though my parents were decidedly backing their candidate, Kennedy (as was I – as if I knew why I was supporting him), I told her I chose Nixon so she would like me more. I figured a harmless white lie, if it brought me closer to Iris, was perfectly excusable in the grand scheme of things. Her parents even had a Nixon sign in their front yard near the school. Pansies were carefully spaced just outside the picket fence as her sparkly Georgian eyes flashed at me when she recognized we'd supported the same candidate. Her parents were from the deep south and, as such, firmly conservative. I often walked her to her picket fenced home, which was in the opposite direction from where we lived. She knew I liked her. More than any other girl, she had the fire. It was in her eyes and in her step. I loved the life that was alive in her. And though we never spoke of it, we were both thinking about marriage. That marriage included a house like her parent's house with a white picket fence and pansies. It included two children and it included dancing. I wanted to watch her dance for the rest of my life. I wondered if her ponytail would always flip from shoulder to shoulder as she danced.

For Iris Stevens, however, this sudden proclaiming of my love of classical music marked me as an "undesirable". That fatal music report marked our courtship with a damning red-rubber-stamp of disapproval. Clunk, went the thunderous stamp. That deafening and officious thump. The marriage was off. I discovered this as I was making up a song about her during recess. While the girls hop-scotched on one side of the playground and the boys tether-balled their way through recess on the other side, I stood squarely in the middle of the playground and between the worlds of the two games as the wind billowed the back of my Hop-a-long Cassidy cowboy shirt. The wind rushed in at the sleeves. I stood on the playground feeling the wind caress my face while the shirt flapped against my chest. David Greengard ran up to me to give me the news that cracked open the world of "the broken heart". David was the kid in class that admitted to me that he also loved classical music. I read his lips as he mouthed the words. He looked worried about me. The words themselves became audible seconds after they dropped around me like bombs on the playground. Wham, went the house with the picket fence. The 'Vote for Nixon' sign exploded sending splinters into the sky above the pansies. And the children, I felt sure we'd have after we were married, faded into a vaporous dust near the tether ball pole as kids merrily played as if nothing out of the ordinary had happened. The playground, once filled with color and the gleeful clatter of children's voices, was now a gray battleground pock marked with smoldering earth and shrapnel. Iris had packed up her freckles and white Bobbie socks and left me to wilt on the playground. The recess bell rang and I had no desire to go back to class. I, instead, would flare my arms allowing my Hop-a-long Cassidy shirt to bellow like a sail thrusting me up and airborne over the school fence. I'd fly over the rows of tract homes. Over the alfalfa fields and orange groves. Over the telephone poles. Guiding a careful landing in front of our house and, slipping through the front door and into my bedroom, I would unceremoniously pull the sheet over my head and softly...die.

Iris Stevens didn't like me anymore because I liked classical music.

The spring in her step during our Friday afternoon square dances was no longer springing for me. They were probably springing for another boy that shared her love of Bill Haley and the Comets, the Big Bopper and Elvis. They would dance with a spring in both their steps. She would marry him. The Rock and Roll man of her dreams would sell insurance and she'd wait at home for him with the music from the radio playing loudly as she danced in the kitchen and giggled that cute giggle of hers.

As for me, I had proclaimed myself an outsider. A heretic. And what's more, I was utterly un-hip. Sure, I liked Bill Haley and the rest of them, but I also loved classical music. And the music that wrapped itself around my emotions, was invariably of the classical sort. The musical figures that would often just pop in my head were like the transporting melodic lines of Chopin and Haydn.

If I was going to be liked (love, at that point seemed out of the question), things had to change. And they did. The wonder of music, birds, clouds, nature and the moon, had been supplanted by a more urgent imperative. Social survival.

Mom's Survival

My father would stay later and later at work with an eye for making more money to take the edge off of the financial strain. My mother would give up all of her dreams of being an artist in the name of being a mother and wife instead. She was, at times, dangerously unhappy. It was up to me to keep her glued together, I thought. I felt so sorry for her. Sorry that she had no one to talk to. (The world of art, culture and higher education wasn't on my dad's docket and none of her neighborhood friends shared her love of art history.) I was sorry that she had to take care of me, my brother and sister. If it hadn't have been for us, maybe they could have been happy somewhere. Maybe on an Island somewhere.

I kept the family together. It was my job. Because if my mother was happy, everyone could rest a little easier. The house was able to breathe. I was glad to do it, because as long as she was happy, I had a mother. We all did. When she was depressed, the house was a tricky place to be. Underneath her moodiness was an interesting person, so I rolled with it.

I would spend hours talking to my mother. I'd encourage her to talk to me about art history and world religions. I was a young therapist with endless time on his hands listening to my mother's philosophizing. She seemed to know endlessly about things that no one else seemed the least bit interested in. Her love of painting was the Island she went to when mothering became, simply, too boring or too predictable. A part of me believed that I'd be granted special dispensation and not have to do homework if, somehow, I helped my mother cope. Alas, not a chance. Two things were emerging as inescapable in life: School and Homework.

I thought, sometimes, my dad was afraid of her. Afraid of what she'd do. Would she leave? Would she just up and leave? Would she yell and yell until she lost her voice? My mother was like the phases of the moon. She was always changing. Sometimes she shone brightly and other times she'd disappear. It would even happen with a kind of predictable regularity.

I knew that if I didn't keep her intact, I would die. Dying was out of the question so I would get her talking.

It always made both of us feel better.

~

My dad was a little suspicious of the relationship I had with my mom. He wondered what on earth she had in common with a pip-squeak like me, but he also knew when to leave well enough alone. And he did.

My relationship with my mother changed as I left elementary school.

CHAPTER 8

Middle School

WHEN WE ALL turned 12 and 13 in school, everything was different. The girls were no longer giggly and playful. I found I could no longer joke with them. Everything evolved into deadly serious. And I wondered what had happened. What happened to the friends that would play at a moment's notice?

I was actually sad about it. Sad, lonely and confused about it. Had a nuclear cloud settled on Los Angeles over the summer and changed everybody? Had the Cuban missile crisis actually escalated into something so absolutely macabre that my parents couldn't bring themselves to tell me about it? I just *knew* that we had all lost something basic. We'd lost something important. We'd shed a skin or something. Maybe everyone had a rough summer. Maybe it had to do with pubic hair or hormones and the fact that most of the girls grew breasts that summer. Maybe growing breasts stole energy from the girls. Maybe puberty came with a price-tag. But it wasn't just the girls, even the boys were distracted and talking differently. I thought maybe the lizard in my dream had something to do with it:

Dream

I was face to face with a lizard. A large, near-human-sized, lizard. He had bitten everyone on our neighborhood block, yet I had somehow avoided the bite by deftly out-maneuvering him. All the other kids who had been bitten appeared less spontaneous and playful. They were just all a bit more subdued and serious since their encounter with the lizard. I was not going to let that happen to me.

"What are you so afraid of?" asked the lizard as he had me cornered between the wall over-grown with ivy and the driveway of our house in the Valley.

He sat back on his tail so I could see his slick and shiny scaly blue underbelly. Immodest and matter of fact, he dropped his reptilian stealth with me and decided to just ... chat.

"What is the big deal here," he asked bluntly. "I just want to inflict this harmless bite...and you see everyone else here on the block...they're all fine...going about their business...absolutely nothing the matter here...what are you so afraid of?" the lizard asked calmly with a kind of academician's reserve. "What makes you so different from everybody else? No one else put up a fuss."

"I don't want it." I protested.

"You don't want it. I see. And why not?" he said, narrowing his eyes on me.

"I don't want to be bitten *just* because you've bitten everyone else," I countered. "I don't want to be like everyone else. I'm not *like* everyone else."

"Not good enough, I'm afraid. You *are* like everyone else."

Those words were like a stake through my heart. That middle class proverb had been packed and sealed into my brain by the time I was six. "You're no different than anybody else," I'd hear. And I would think, 'Then why aren't more people thinking that school and hospitals and adults are insane?'

"Stop daydreaming and come back to the here and now. Your excuses are silly, commonplace and predictable," he said with a patience that seethed with a subterranean malevolence. "And, it's not good enough," he added.

"Well, it's gonna be good enough and that's that." I said.

"It doesn't hurt," he cooed. His eyes stared fixedly, as only a reptile can, waiting for a sign of weakness...an entry point. "Frankly, it's now or it's later, it doesn't make that big a difference to me," he said uncrossing then crossing his legs. "Everyone ultimately gives in."

"No?" I asked.

"No, what?"

"It doesn't hurt?" I continued.

"Of course it doesn't hurt. Unless you're a sissy." he countered.

"I'm not doing it," I said.

I was standing resolute, but he was apparently unfazed. He was completely relaxed and confident that he would get his way. He was used to getting his way. Then as impatience got the better of him and, doing his best to contain his annoyance, he sneaked a glance at his lizard watch as if he needed to keep to a schedule:

"Oh, come on now. You've avoided me for long enough. Stop playing your little...look-at-me-I'm-special game. Just stop it. STOP it. You're holding out because you're a miserable little shit. Now, *come* on. Look around you. Look at these other children. Any of them complaining? No. Everyone's fine. But, Mr. Special, here, needs to be treated differently because *he's* different. He's..."

Catching himself, he smiled his syrupy reptile smile.

"It doesn't hurt?" I asked.

His eyes widened slightly thinking he might have me on this one.

"Oh, maybe for a half second, it's nothing." he continued like a doctor dismissing a kids fear of a polio shot.

"Now or later...'has to happen eventually?" I asked.

"Yesss," the lizard said calmly his eyes now hypnotic.

"OK," I said, "do your worst."

I woke up.

–

The girls were now holding their notebooks and books in front of them as if they were hiding behind something as they'd walk. Their notebooks were, now, no longer at their sides like the year before. And there was the look on their faces that suggested they'd been bitten by the lizard. They had a serious and, at times, anxious look on their faces like they were constantly late for class. It seemed something had taken possession of them.

These wonderful friends of mine from the 1st and 2nd grade, now in the 7th grade, had vanished. They'd been whisked away by a thief in the night. I couldn't talk to them because they were always late to go somewhere. The girls were pulling their tight skirts down as if someone had dressed them in a skirt entirely too short. And as they'd tug on their skirts, they looked vexed and uncomfortable: victims of a skirt too short. Victims of the lizard. Damned lizard.

I'd sometimes even be daydreaming about girls in class when suddenly the bell would ring and I'd have to walk to my next class like the girls did – books in front of me.

The other boys became more cruel since that summer. They'd spit (sometimes on me) and push and punch. The language, the stride, the movements all got more coarse. And, if I made my way from one class to another with my books in front of me, instead of getting a knowing "I understand you, brother" glance, I got chided mercilessly for carrying my books like a girl.

Linda

Linda had breasts. Linda had been bitten by the lizard, but she hadn't completely let go of that little girl inside of her. Her rough edges and lack of refinement suggested that she might have been from the other side of the tracks but she wasn't like the other girls. She had still managed a kind of vulnerability about her. She had written "Michael" maybe 200 times in a flowing cursive on a piece of notebook paper until it was completely covered with my name. On the other side of the paper, she continued writing my name until about a third of the way down the paper where she began writing "Linda" until the astigmatic and repetitive long-hand filled the rest of the page. She shyly handed it to me between 2nd and 3rd period.

I wrote "Linda" on a piece of paper maybe 50 times just to show her that I was thankful that she'd reached out to me. And, well, that I liked her too. Because she liked me.

Maybe she didn't dance like Iris did. Maybe she didn't have the lightness in her step or the fire like Iris did. Maybe she didn't have Iris's quick wit. Maybe she didn't have the white fence squaring her family's front yard, but she seemed to care for me. And that was what was important now. And she was a girl. A girl becoming a woman. And for however long it must have taken to write our names on that paper, she seemed to want to do things with me. I promised myself not to talk to her about Johannes Brahms. Besides which, Brahms was sinking beneath my interest horizon anyway. He belonged to a world of long ago that coexisted with social suicide. He, along with all the other friends I'd made in our Elementary School library: Beethoven, Haydn, Schubert, Handel, Bach and Chopin.

I handed her the piece of paper on which I'd written her name. She looked squarely in my eyes and slipped her hand into mine.

"That was easy," I thought to myself. "I'm starting to get the hang of this thing,"

And although Linda was a blonde Caucasian, she hung out with a near comical bunch of rough and tumble Mexican kids. And seeing that she liked me, they accepted me because she'd "punch them" if they didn't. They were "Greasers". I didn't know what a Greaser was. But I was going to become one of them.

I saved up enough money with my newspaper delivery job to get a Pendleton wool shirt and pointy black boots. I styled my hair the way they did and I was baptized into this family of Greasers after walking through these underground sewers accessible, at the time, from the Los Angeles "wash"[1]. With Linda's hand in mine we walked for hours with a group of a dozen Latino kids through a labyrinthine network of sewer systems with a few inches of water sloshing between our feet in the dark tunnels.

One of the other girls took my hand as well and asked why my hands were so rough.

"Because I work out on the horizontal bar," I said. "I do gymnastics."

---

[1] The LA River starts in the San Fernando Valley, in the Simi Hills and Santa Susana Mountains, and flows through Los Angeles County from Canoga Park nearly 48 miles to Long Beach.

"Ohhhhh," she said, approvingly. She looked at Linda. They both held my sand-paper hands.

I wondered why Linda had allowed me to, however briefly, hold the hand of another girl. I just figured it was the family way. For they were like family. I liked this family. They took care of each other and cared for each other in ways that, apparently, even real families didn't.

I had arrived. I was now accepted. I was accepted in this small sector of society inhabited by the Greasers. And things were looking up.

I had the right clothes. I had a girlfriend with breasts. A girlfriend that held my hand. A girlfriend that would flatten any of these guys that didn't like me. And I had the hair, with the help of styling gel.

And the hair was important. Everyone knew that. The straighter, the better.

Of High Bars and Swinging Rings

I developed my skills on the horizontal bar and swinging rings so that I got noticed. Releasing the metal rings after pumping hard to get swinging high, I'd float around myself doing a lay-out back flip. This impressed Linda. This impressed the Greasers. It gave me credibility. It made me more masculine in their eyes. What is more, I loved the feeling. It reminded me of a far away sensation of weightlessness. It seemed, at once, edgy and euphoric as flying through the air upside down profoundly intensified my awareness of the moment with the air whistling by my ears. It was me on the playground with a billowing Hop-along Cassidy cowboy shirt; it was me flying high above my school in my dreams; it was me picking concord grapes as I lie on my back, without a care in the world, on a lazy late summer's day at the neighborhood farm...all rolled in to one.

I got to know the other Latino guys and liked them a lot. They did what the Caucasian boys didn't, they laughed and had an easier way about them. Though they could appear menacing at times, they still had a childlike vulnerability to them that was alive. They were imaginative and playful in ways that were foreign to me at the time. The ones that didn't sniff modeling glue were really funny and good guys and they had now approved of my relationship with Linda. And Linda didn't need to protect me anymore. I'd become one of the family. My ability to fly through the air made them all respect me and also made them a little afraid of me. ("...if he can do that, what *else* can he do?")

Hollywood

Everything seemed to be going along so well until we moved closer to Los Angeles. It made my father's commute to downtown Los Angeles much easier by cutting travel time in half. I dropped my Greaser persona. It didn't fly in Hollywood. It was more a Valley thing then a Hollywood thing. I got another paper route, delivering newspapers at 4:00 a.m. every morning in the summer. Linda was now a vague memory. I wondered whose name she was writing on a piece of notebook paper now. I wondered whose hand she held walking in the underground Los Angeles Basin Wash. I wondered who she was protecting. And, I wondered if she wondered the same about me.

I tried to be a part of a social group of other kids my age. Always looking for the key that would give me access, I continued my gymnastics to gain credibility and respect. So immersed was I in the need for acceptance, that all else faded away. Acceptance was a slippery and foreign notion. I knew I had to "do" something without knowing exactly what it was. In fact, doing things acceptably became of paramount importance. It kept me looking and acting "like everyone else". The lizard had gotten his way. And the lizard was happy about it.

A part of me was wanting to go to sleep. I wanted to sleep and think of the girl that sang opposite me in choir. The girl with the bleached blonde hair and and feminine anatomy pushing up against her choir gown during our choral performance.

I became interested in the mystery that was the female. The mystery that was the female body. I still wanted the contact with skin and the dizzying effect it had on me. If only I could be lying in the grass, talking informally with the bleached blonde from choir, everything would magically be ok. Everything would be right again. I could relax. Lying down in nature and out of school, I could relax.

The Occult

The sense of 'other' made itself known to me in my fevered hunger for everything 'unseen'. Just as I'd occasionally look at the unfocused space between me and the sky as a flurry of translucent, and somehow conscious, activity darted about, I was also drawn to hypnosis and the Ouija board. Freud and Jung replaced the musical companion I found in Brahms.

Taking it all very seriously, I learned how to induce the hypnotic state at age 15 and experimented on the most willing subject I could find. I regressed her to infancy and in subsequent sessions, to her experience before birth and to a previous life. Always pushing the limit, I progressed her 70 years into the future. She described things that would be, incredibly, invented 30 years later. I dabbled so much in the occult that I came to have a foot in two worlds: The seen and the unseen. And because I could sense the incipience and slow inexorability in being swallowed up by the unseen, I stopped it all together. I withdrew the foot from the unseen world and made the conscious decision to stay in the world of everyone else. To stay in the seen world. To stay in the world of the lizard. Straddling two worlds was too much to ask and I didn't want to once again risk social ostracism.

It was around that time that I went to sleep.

Me boarding a jet to Europe - 1970

CHAPTER 9

The Sleep

I REFINED THE science of being liked by polishing my presentation with every passing fad du jour. In a word. I was likable. Unassuming. People saw me as having an easy-going way about me. Like my father, I managed to help people feel good about themselves. With a left-of-center sense of humor, I was like an irrepressibly winsome 16-year-old insurance salesman. And though I didn't sell insurance, I should have. I would have been retired by now.

I had no idea, however, what I was really doing. Nor, did I have any idea at what price it would come. I was attempting to assure my own survival, though, by improving my packaging. I needed to be a 'good boy', a convivial, fun-to-be-around-boy. Having made approval a big part of my own self-concept, every kid I knew had the power to make me feel accepted...or not. And in ways, too numerous to mention, social survival was survival pure and simple for me. And the difference between socially surviving and not, as a teenager, was quite simply the difference between life and death. And that was the way it stayed for a while. If I wasn't liked or accepted, life became a lonely and desolate proposition. When I was feeling accepted or appreciated, I felt better about myself as if I was part of something larger – and I was doing it right.

The solitary and self-possessed path was a desolate and dusty road I was unprepared, and too unskilled, to travel.

In short, the focus had shifted from the wonder of the "Ooom" to: "Are my socks matching the pants I'm wearing because if they're not, I'll stick out and be un-cool. I'll be unlovable."

I actually, once in the 10th grade, found that I'd put on a brown sock and a black sock in the dim light of my room on an early winter's morning. I discovered this at school and was horrified at the realization. Panicked, I phoned home and told my Dad what I'd done pleading with him that he bring the sock to make what I was wearing a matched pair. In his brilliance, he suggested I see it another way:

"Why don't you just make a joke about it?" he asked.

"Whaddya mean, joke about having two different color socks? What's so funny about that?" I asked, panicked.

"Use it as a way to start a conversation. Make it funny. Just go with it," he said with a voice that told me there was a twinkle in his voice stretching out to me over the telephone line.

He always had a twinkle in his eye and a twinkle in his voice. To this day, I don't know how he did it. I was too young and too stressed to understand the gist of what he was saying. This was one of the golden moments when my father was passing his wisdom on to me which I was to appreciate years later.

For me though, social conformity had eclipsed the importance of the birds in the trees. It was more important than the moon. More important than family. More important than anything. The God of conformity swept through my life like a hurricane unseating even the most tender appreciation for nature and all things wondrous and magical. I was an obedient disciple of all conformist idolatry. Nowhere was the crush of conformity more important than in high school – particularly as an underclass-man. My father did, though, bring me the sock to make a matched pair.

High School was a popularity contest I was determined to be a part of. Probably the thoughts of being isolated smacked of the time spent in the strange solitary confinement that was the hospital experience. And that was a chapter I couldn't repeat. The harrowing reminders of loneliness and isolation seemed like the cruelest of punishments for not kneeling at the feet of the cultural golden calf.

Yet, while the outside personality presentation was polished, the inside nagged with an emptiness begging for attention. But, as long as no one noticed the inside…and how could they?...I'd be OK. I'd have a girlfriend that would make me feel normal and accepted and happy and a part of the wild, beautiful world of youth. And it did – for a while.

Like a speed boat slicing through the water and slowing to a stop for the voluminous wake to at last catch up to the stern of the boat, in college the illusion of being popular swelled and burst. The popularity, so hard-won in high school, vanished and I was back at square one. The at once daunting, vexing and confounding question of "Who am I?" knocked at my door. What if I'd answered the door and found that I'd been a complete phoney and that there was nothing under the facade? It was too frightening a prospect. I wouldn't answer the door.

College

Short stints at being a box boy and delivering chicken made me only want to hop a freight train, which I did. Because my parents didn't want to see me "hit bottom" they suggested I move out. I wanted to move out anyway but didn't have the courage to actually do it.

With a surreal suddenness, I found myself living in the Salvation Army in San Jose. I was 19 years old. Although, I had to swallow hard the first day I waited to pay my dollar to sleep there for the night, I learned something valuable:

Things are rarely what they seem.

The Salvation Army in and of itself wasn't such a bad place. It was a rude awakening after living at home, to be sure. It was frightening to be alone and without friends and family. But it wasn't that bad.

At that time, San Jose, California was a small town. Entertainment consisted of cruising up and down 1st and 2nd streets on a Friday winter's night with the car windows rolled down and the heater blasting with enough heat to warm a small community. San Jose was a waste land. And for many months, the Salvation Army was my home. Built low to the ground, alternately with brick, mortar and stucco and spectacularly featureless like an over-sized tract home, the Salvation Army was home to drifters and fringe-types, of which I was one.

"Why are you homeless? Why don't you just get a job and settle in some-where," I asked a guy about 3 years older than I was.

"I don't wanna do the madness," Joel said.

Joel was clean and fit but walked with a slovenly gait with his head pitched forward suggesting that he was carrying an oxen's yoke. His jeans were slung low on his hip, his lean frame didn't give his pants a chance in hell for staying at his waist. He was always reading a book, and when he'd finish reading, he'd throw it up in the air as the pages flapped in wild protest at the ungratefulness of its reader.

"But you're smart and..."

"...and that's why I'm not part of this mess," he said as he looked to one side where the thin and faded patch of grass bordered the fence lining the railroad tracks. He looked down at his shoes.

He spent a lot of time looking at his shoes, I guess to make sure that they were still on his feet. Shoes were an issue at the Salvation Army. You slept with them under your pillow. That's what I was told the first night I was there.

"You always sleep with yer shoes under yer pillow, 'cause if'n anyone wants 'em, 'n they're under yer bed, they's good as gone," one of the "Sally" veterans warned me. And I needed my shoes because walking was something I did a lot of. A lot of the indigents looked at their shoes. I figured they also needed reminding that they had their feet on the ground.

Joel was different from many of the other guys there. Most of them smelled of old sweat and dirt and were alcoholics with deep canyons etched in their foreheads. I'd figured it was because of the smoking, drinking, harsh weather, and carrying the weight of the world. All that abuse showed up on their faces like a relief map of Canyonlands National Park. They were a rag-tag assemblage of misfits – even cartoon-ish sometimes. There were drug addicts, cross-dressers, psychos and guys, simply, "down on their luck". Even an occasional woman would stay in the room separate from the men's dormitories. She'd be, presumably, fleeing a physically abusive relationship with a few snot-faced kids in tow. The guys would ogle as she'd walk hurriedly to her room.

"Hey, princess. How's about you 'n me goin' to the ..."

And even before they'd managed to finish voicing their invitation made unintelligible by alcohol, she'd hastily shut the door.

But, somehow fascinatingly, there were sages that mingled among these frayed souls that found sanctuary in the nightly arms of the "Sally". And they drifted among the homeless unnoticed and indistinguishable from the rest. And Joel was one of those sages. He looked the part of a street person, but was decidedly in a world apart.

"Yeah, well what're *you* doin' here," he said out of nowhere looking me up and down. "You don't belong here," he sneered.

"Now I do," I managed.

And I did. I had no money. Nowhere to go. And no friends. I was at the bottom of the barrel at 19 years old. No prospects. No light at the end of the tunnel. I'd hit bottom just as my parents had feared.

I was skinny. Wiry. And I was starting to take on the 'look' of the homeless. The battle-weary thousand-yard stare was moving in on my eyes with the unstoppable inexorability of a San Francisco morning fog, and I'd barely been homeless a month. I was to stay another 3 months before scraping together enough money to pay for an apartment. But, sages or not, they all had one thing in common:

They couldn't do the madness. Living on the hazed and alcoholic seams of a consensus reality seemed to suit them just fine.

And I could only guess that the madness was made up of the inhuman stress of just making a living. The stress of living up to expectations. The stress of getting ahead and staying ahead of the bills. Or the crazy stress of losing someone close. And in that way, homelessness was a type of latter day foreign legion. And the 'look' was the scarlet letter distinguishing those on the outside of society from those on the inside. While I regarded these guys warily at times, something about them made me want to know what made them tick. How had they gotten so disenchanted with living life like 'everyone else' that they'd end up in a homeless shelter? What had happened to their families, girlfriends and friends? What happened to them?

I learned a lot from Joel. We'd go on walks that would take us from one end of San Jose to the other. We actually tried finding buried treasure once. I had no idea where he got the map or what the hell kind of treasure we were even looking for. But there was nothing much else to do. And treasure was good. So we talked about the madness while we looked for treasure...fully expecting to find it.

Joel maintained that you play the game, or you don't. For him, the cost of playing the game came with too high a price. So, he hopped freight trains from town to town. And each town merely was a backdrop for the next book he read. He told me this or that person was completely full of themselves, referring to celebrities or politicians. And I couldn't disagree. I couldn't disagree with anything he said. He saw through all the trappings of societal contrivance: The pathological egoity. The need to wear the job-face, or the family-face. He was pretty much opposed to having to wear any kind of face. He had had it with the fast train of what was rapidly becoming corporate America. He felt it was dehumanizing and nuts.

I felt he could easily go back to a 'sane and comfortable' life any time he wanted. He could be with one of his brothers and share their wealth. He could go back to the woman he, probably, left behind and live a life that others expected of him. A cozy life. A warm body at night and during the day after work, he could shuttle the kids to baseball practice.

He just didn't want to. And, damn it, no one was going to make him.

I found the roadblocks to getting a job too numerous and insurmountable having no address, and if I simply referred to the Salvation Army as my address, my application wasn't given a minute's consideration. San Jose State was no exception. If I had no acceptable address, the school would not allow me to attend. And, I was dead set on not being drafted into a crazy war in Southeast Asia. A student deferment was the only logical way out.

After making enough money, finally working *for* the Salvation Army, I'd gotten myself in an apartment. The only bit of furniture was a bed, a dresser, a kitchen table and a bicycle leaned against the wall.

There was a young married couple that lived down the hall. They were American-picture-perfect. She always smiled. They were also students at San Jose State. She didn't like listening to Simon and Garfunkle because she found their music depressing. They were mature. They were adult for their age.

There was Chester, the black dissident, who also went to San Jose State. He set the record straight on what it was to be a man. And a man could only prove himself in one place: "...in da bayed."

"Nothing else is important? A woman can't like you because you're thoughtful or creative or..."

"Mmmm mm," he insisted. "S'all about da bed..."

"That just seems so..."

"...I know what it seems so. But, das what is," he said.

He studied my face.

"Don't you look at me like that. I'm older 'n you 'n I know."

He, himself, was a little horrified at just how banal it all was. There was a thoughtful and sensitive being wrapped inside of the dissident that Chester projected. But he looked at life and all of its weirdnesses with a kind of resignation – a kind of victim-laced (although partially true) plight of the Afro-American.

"The Black man doesn't have a chance. We live in a white man's world. We dream about white women. We dream about all things white. And we say we're proud of bein' Black. Shi-it."

He set me up with one of his black girlfriends so I could see for myself. In the vertical world, I didn't fit in. In the horizontal world, I did. It was as if I was in the world of 'nothing to hide' and there I could relax. And in love-making, I was free. Free from my neuroses of feeling so radically different from everyone and everything else. I was free like a tree. Free like the sky. It was a place outside of the busy-ness of being human.

Days later, while hanging a window shade in my bathroom, a metal bracket shot off the spring-loaded stem of the shade and glanced off my eye. I needed to be on my back and in the hospital for a few weeks with both eyes bandaged to minimize movement of the eye so the retina wouldn't detach. Being blind was a humbling experience, but when I was back in my apartment and I removed the gauze from both eyes weeks later, the world was revealed to me as if for the first time. I watched the soap as it glistened, reflecting the overhead bathroom light while taking my first bath since getting out of the hospital. Colors were rich, deep and brilliant. The light reflected off objects in ways I'd never seen before. It was orgasmic. Exciting. A tingling sense of discovery gripped me. It was like I'd never used my eyes before.

If I'd deprived all my senses, would it be like being *alive* for the first time?

During that semester at San Jose State, I discovered the meaning of "existential angst" and that definition drove me to reading every book I could get my hands on promising to reveal something about this existential craziness that

I was now experiencing. Maybe I'd talked to Joel too much. Maybe he got me thinking too much. I felt that at the bottom of the angst, for me, was a schism between my "personality" and whatever remained of my essential self that I'd left behind a long time ago. Joel had opened a door for me. And I was, with the curiosity of a scientist, walking through that door. And I was studying what was on the other side.

While in school, I found myself increasingly disinterested in my classes and became a voracious reader. Typically, reading a book a day, I'd begin before 5 in the morning and finish late that night, somehow sandwiching a class or two in between. With waning interest in finishing my third year of college and an increasingly keen curiosity in knowing more about life itself, I wanted to go to Europe. Most of the books I'd read used Europe as a backdrop. Many of the writers were, themselves, European. Europe had something that San Jose didn't. It had something that Los Angeles didn't. What Europe had, I wanted to know more about because I sensed that my mental survival was dependent on it.

I made a deal with my parents to pay them room and board for a few months while working enough to pay for a one-way passage to Europe. I'd asked that they do this one last thing for me and to just allow me to stay at their house again so I could save money to fly one-way to London. A week before taking the flight, my high school love reappeared in my life. Becca was the woman whose memory I couldn't shake and had remained in love with for the past few years. Seeing her awakened something passionate in me. I wanted Becca more than Iris. I wanted her more than any woman I'd ever met. All the songs that arose in my chest were about her. Every song on the radio, I made about her. Every romantic fantasy was about her. The fire for her was more than I was able to express and the day after seeing her I had, what could have only been, a nervous break down. Alternately shaking and crying uncontrollably, the psychiatrist at L.A. County Mental Hospital said I shouldn't go on this trip to Europe. I was too unstable. Recommending a mood drug and twice weekly visits to a psychiatrist, I decided to go to Europe anyway. Bewildered, my parents watched as I was engulfed by the rippling waves of heat rising off the tarmac at the Burbank airport. With every possession I owned on my back, I boarded the silver bird of salvation on that hot, dry, 2nd of July day. But London was only the jumping off point. Me and my pack, bought at the army surplus store, and my confused and broken heart were off to Hermann Hesse's, Ernest Hemingway's, Thomas Mann's, Jean-Paul

Sartre's, Lawrence Durrell's, and Somerset Maugham's ...Europe! And I had absolutely no idea where to go or what to expect.

This was where Hemingway's character fought in Spain. Where Hermann Hesse and Thomas Mann and Jean Paul Sartre battled their demons. Where Freud and Jung paved new territory in psychiatry. This was where Brahms and Chopin and Haydn lived and composed! I wanted to battle every one of my demons just like they did. I wanted to be an artist in Europe. I wanted to be like Brahms or Henry Miller. For me, there was no difference between them. They all dizzily and singularly pursued their life's quest. Damn the cultural-norm-torpedos! I would be a Bohemian.

Hitch-hiking, I often fell into other fringe elements like the ones in San Jose's Salvation Army. With the European displaced persons, like the nerds in high school, I found that the idea of societal madness wasn't a uniquely American viewpoint. After hitch-hiking for a year, once again, without a place to live and down to the end of my resources, I briefly hung out with this colorful roving band of homeless people living beneath bridges along the River Seine in Paris. They'd fend for one another like family. I found this profoundly moving. Actually, I hadn't experienced this highly intensified sense of family anywhere else. They were selfless and had nothing. But what they did have, they were willing...more than willing, to share with the others. Like a nomadic band of gypsies, they made money here and there only as they needed it. What is more, they always shared whatever they happened on. They were like a circus family. The family that none of them ever really had, I supposed. They were like the Latinos I knew in the Valley. The homeless guys in San Jose. What did they all have in common?: They all lived on the outer limits of cultural acceptability.

So, I posed the same question to the apparent ringleader:

"What're you doing here? You seem really bright. Couldn't you get a job and settle somewhere?"

He handed me half of his baguette as we sat on a cement stoop overlooking the Seine idly flowing by: condoms, food wrappers and paper cups bobbing in the water marbling with silt and dirt, "I'm not going to pretend to adjust to insanity...the wars...the factories...no, never." He wiped the clinging bread crumbs from the sides of his mouth with his sleeve, looked down at his shoes and continued. "I'm much happier living this way than living in that world...their world."

I was reminded of the wonderfully poetic anti-war film, *The King of Hearts* where the insane asylum housed all the 'crazy' pacifists. And, not unlike all Bohemians everywhere, they ask the eternal question:

Who's crazy, here?

Like in middle school and high school and like in life: I always gravitated to those living on the seams of the norm. They all had another thing in common, they were stubbornly holding on to something that they felt was very vitally their own. It was something that was too important, too essential, to give away. Without it, they would be worthless. Without it, they couldn't live with themselves.

~

(Even now, as I travel, I meet some of the most interesting people. Many of them seem united to make the planet a more livable, sustainable and just place. They travel from country to country meeting people of other cultures as if doing research. They want no part of a life that is simply consumed in surviving. Consumed in consuming. And, above all, they see the ridiculousness in living a life that is fraught with the stress in living for this nebulous 'future time' when, with retirement, they'd be free. Free to travel. Free to enjoy life. Free to do the things they've always wanted to do. It's a sweet seduction for most. But, for those intrepid travelers I've met, it's the grandest of tricks.)

In short:

The illusion of the linear passage of time and the time relegated to working, has a built-in cultural motivator: Working until we have 'enough'. We work and work some more until we can be free to enjoy all that life holds for us (Arbeit Macht Frei?!).

~

I traveled with that back pack for the better part of two years to nearly every country in Europe. I was looking for a woman to make it all better. I was looking for a woman to make me feel whole. I was always looking. I was looking to find who I was without my family, friends and country. I was looking for meaning outside the commonly accepted reasons for being alive.

I turned 21 in Europe. On a certain cold winter's day in Stuttgart, where I'd enrolled myself in a Rudolph Steiner school of Anthroposophy, the thoughts in my head were running like wild steeds that had been spooked. I had to get outside of my thoughts. I felt like someone going crazy. I went sprinting out of the school's compound as the cold afternoon air burned at my nostrils and lungs. I ran as hard as I could for as far as I could so I could feel something real and get out of my head. I weaved between old German ladies walking on the sidewalk spying me carefully. Between mothers pushing prams, I ran avoiding the frozen patches on the ground and sidewalk. My feet flew over the ground beneath me as my body began to ache from the running and sting with the cold. The icy air bit at my ears. My muscles burned and ultimately gave up. My body could do no more. Collapsing on the sidewalk, winded, nauseated and faint, I noticed:

Cloud.

Sky.

Tree.

Birds!

Waiting for the dizzying swirl of trees above my head to stand still, my reeling awareness became focused like a laser on this miraculous moment outside the prison of my thoughts. Sounds became clear and bell-like. The cold had a bracing, fresh chill of aliveness within it. My brain, filled with oxygen, buzzed with vitality. With a mighty and deft sweep of a hand across the table of my thoughts, the preconceived notions, beliefs and ideas dropped to the floor and, showing their true fragility, shattered into a million pieces.

I had a glimpse of a world I'd been looking for ever since I'd first intoned the sound:

"Ooom".

I lay there like a crazy man, my arms and legs out-stretched like DiVinci's Vitruvian Man staring like a star-crossed lover offering his body to the sky above. And, as if nothing else existed...

...I laughed.

CHAPTER 10

Reawakened in the Rag Business

I RETURNED TO THE states earnestly convinced that I should make enough money to attend the University at Strasbourg and major in French and minor in German. I'd make money as quickly as I could doing whatever I had to do and blitz back to Europe.

After a year of getting over the culture shock of being back in Los Angeles, at the behest of my father, I slipped into the garment business. Whatever shine I was able to inject into my well-oiled high school persona, I was able to reconstitute and incorporate into being a textile salesman. The textile business was a great two-fer for me. I was able to get to know the world of my father (and finally get to know *him* at the same time), and it was a formidable testing ground to see if I could fit into ANY sector of society after living on the fringes for so long. I had good reason to doubt if I could ever fit into any social system.

The other salesmen in downtown Los Angeles were variously funny, cut-throat, clever, a New York outcast, cunning, intellectual, a crook, an actor, beggar or all of the above. And, at that time, 90% Jewish. This was a new world for me. Yiddish-isms were an active part of everyday business dealings. The 'game' was played between the manufacturer's buyer and the salesmen.

It was a stunningly detailed and time-honored game. The lunches, the drinking, the schmoozing was all part of a culture about which I hadn't the vaguest notion . Because, I think, I was so very clueless about the 'game', I had a high entertainment value for the dress designers and buyers. I was utterly naïve to the ways of the game and I was seen as one who was both innocent and cute. So, because the cute moniker was handed to me, I built on it. I acted even more innocent than I was – more of a Goy than I actually was. I'd even hear laughing in my wake as I'd leave a buyer's office. I had absolutely no business, haggling or negotiating acumen and I had no business even trying. I was a novelty for buyers and garment designers that were used to the tried and true lace, button and fabric salesman sales pitch. I was the curly-haired, honest-by-default, non-New York-transplant. I would get the female designers laughing so hard, they would buy from me just so I'd come back to break up the predictability of their day. So I got little orders here and there. The *really* big orders were negotiated by the heavy hitters that actually *did* know what they were doing.

By accident or design, I became relatively successful for a newcomer. I became so successful that, this kid who'd only two years prior been living on less than $50 a month in Europe, had now paid cash for a sports car and was earning many times more than his father. Driving away from the car lot with the top down on my new red convertible, I laughed on the Ventura Freeway because I just felt so damned good. Curly locks dancing in the wind, I felt that I finally understood this whole mystery. I'd had the cues down. I knew how to fool them. I could fool them all into thinking that I fit in. And now I looked the part -- in spades. Some of the older married salesmen looked at me with loathing and contempt. Others looked at me with envy and amusement. Even my father had mixed emotions about my success. I'd had my own office with 3 employees and the place was always humming with activity.

The other salesmen mused endlessly over my mysterious and meteoric success. What had I been doing? Was I schtupping all the female designers to get orders? Was I really a gigolo posing as a "rag salesman"?

And while I did go to bed with some of the designers I worked with, I got most of my orders because I was simply funny. And everyone likes funny. People go out of their way to have "funny" in their day. I sported a mustache and, at times, sun-glasses. I'd stepped into a role and was milking it for all it was worth.

There was a part of me that I kept uniquely to myself, however. It was the part that wrote 2-hour journal entries every day. It was the part that learned piano and quietly learned how to write songs. It was the part that was still walking across the tarmac looking for something deeper. It was the part that studied Russian, Mandarin, German and French. I became, literally, two people: a polished social navigator and a restless and interior lone wolf. And the two managed to co-exist side-by-side. But the journal entries spoke to an increasing disquietude in this split. One side viewed the other contemptuously.

"You're depressive and anti-social," scoffed the socialite.

"You're a shallow hedonist," derided the artist.

The artist self was looking for expression and it would not tolerate being brushed aside by a mere social butterfly of a garment salesman.

The split was actually functional. Downtown Los Angeles was for the laughably slick button and lace salesman and my rental at Manhattan Beach was for the brooding sensitive artist navigating existential depravity. I could've finessed a cooperative relationship between the two, but instead I bought a house and distracted myself no end. Some of those distractions ended up being life-changers.

Vladimir in his Moscow apartment - Dec 1978

CHAPTER 11

Vladimir Vysotsky

A MONG SOME OF the most amazing things that have occurred in this, at once charmed and strange, life of mine is that I've met absolutely amazing people.

Richard sat next to me on a plane while flying back to Germany to meet my former German girlfriend, Elke, with whom I stayed for 8 months alternately on the Greek Island of Santorini and in Stuttgart in 1971. Richard sold computer hardware, at the time, to the Soviets. Richard was Polish and, like most everyone from Europe, multilingual. Though he lived in Southern California, his dealings had him speaking in Polish, Russian and German as he'd travel to those countries. We committed to getting together when our respective trips were over. My visit with Elke was disappointing. We'd simply gone in two entirely different directions to relate to one another anymore. She had continued with her study and practice of pedagogy as we had *both* planned to do in Hamburg, and I had made a sharp left turn to become a salesman. We made radically different life choices and we no longer recognized each other. I'd even venture that she was repulsed by me and my mustache. The thoughtful, and sensitive guy she knew in Greece and Germany had been supplanted by a cocky and bawdy American salesman.

Richard and I promptly met up a month after our respective trips. By all indications he was an enormously successful business man. Jocular and playful, he had what seemed to have eluded many of my American male friends: a very playful sense of the absurd. Because I could meet him on the theater of the absurd, he felt that I should also meet a man he'd recently met while staying in Moscow. This Muscovite and his wife, Marina who lived in Paris, were to be coming to the states and would I mind letting them stay at my house in Pacific Palisades. This was to be Vladimir's first time in the United States. Richard's house, at the time, was spoken for and, besides, I'd get along with them "great". Seldom one to decline a new experience, I agreed.

Vladimir[1] was small and wiry like me. We could have been brothers. Marina[2], born of Russian parents who'd immigrated to Paris, was a beautiful blonde and a working actress in France. It was 1977 and we met with instant, playful, recognition. After a brief getting to know each other on their evening arrival, Vladimir emerged from the downstairs bedroom the next morning and we greeted one another. He approached me like a child. Rocking back and forth like a marionette as he walked, I emitted a high munchkin voice in greeting him. His eyes widened. I did it again. And he walked right up to me to look inside my mouth to see where the sound was coming from.

"Do it again," he begged.

I did it again. Then he tried it. With his low, gravelly voice he was challenged to get into that vocal register. Once again, he looked in my mouth as I did a Mickey Mouse voice. He laughed and once again tried to find the placement in his own voice to do it himself. Fascinated by the sound and where it came from, he was determined to find out how this sound was created. He was captivated by the vocal mechanics of the squeezed munchkin voice. Why did it work? How did a tiny voice come out of a man's voice box. He was a mixture of delighted, intrigued and, like a scientist...obsessed with getting to the simple physics of it.

He gave up on Mickey Mouse, for the moment, and we walked out to the bluff near my house overlooking the Pacific Ocean. Flowers along the sidewalk, that were so characteristic of that neighborhood, filled the air with a heady concert of jasmine and enumerable other flowers as if in a florist's shop. As was so often the case in the early Fall, the sky was a striking clear blue and the colors of the flora were other-worldly.

---

[1] Vladimir Vysotsky (1938–1980), one of the most talented Russian bards.
[2] Marina Vlady won the Best Actress Award at the 1963 Cannes Film Festival for *The Conjugal Bed*.

Approaching the cliff as the ocean revealed more and more of its vast expanse, tears welled in his eyes. He looked earnestly at me and said, "I'm going to spend the whole day here, tomorrow, just looking," he said. He looked out over the panoramic deep blue of the Pacific Ocean and took deep breaths. He breathed in every color, every sensation – every inch of the horizon. For moments afterward he was inward and pensive. We walked the few blocks back to my house in silence. Before we went back in the house, he pulled me aside.

"The first time I went to Paris I saw all the lights. I saw all the activity. And all, all, all of the color. It made me so dizzy I vomited," he said. "There was nothing like this in the Soviet Union," he continued, "it made me crazy and it made me want to cry...from sadness or joy...I didn't know which one." Vladimir took my forearm and again, looking meaningfully into my eyes said, "You live in a paradise here. Do you know this?" He kept staring deeply into my eyes. Pressing my forearm for punctuation, to let me know that the moment was finished, we walked into the kitchen.

My French girlfriend Yvette, who I'd met vacationing near Cannes had come to stay at my house, and Marina were drinking coffee. Volodya (Vladimir) spoke in superlatives about this mythical and vast blue azure jewel beyond the bluffs like a boy recounting his greatest adventure, ever, to his best friend. Marina responded matching his enthusiasm.

We played like children in those few weeks.

There was a very alive, very active, child in all four of us. I abbreviated my work days to spend more time with them. Food was a festival – a circus of ooo's and ahhh's. Walking was an adventure. Driving was an expedition. Swimming in the ocean was an ecstasy too sublime. And, laughing was the staple of life. As Marina wrote in her book[3], and as I am writing in mine: *These were some of the happiest days of our lives.*

Early into his stay he took me aside in the living room and wanted to make something clear to me. "There is no person in the Soviet Union that doesn't know me. I am an actor and a singer," he felt it necessary to explain. "The people, they take my recordings. They copy them 14, 15 – 20 times so all people can have my cassettes."

I was to find out several years, after the fact, just how celebrated he really was. He hadn't exaggerated.

---

[3] *Vladimir, or, Flight Interrupted* (never translated into English)

With his gravelly, throaty and passionate singing voice he sang ballads about the oppression of the Soviets; the suppression of the human spirit; and the fantastic resilience of that same indefatigable human spirit to rise up and fight for its rightful place to exist and to *express* itself. *No* one would have guessed that beneath the powerful bull-frog of a masculine voice, there was a man with more child in him than most. That this man of such colossal talent and artistic stature not only as an actor[4], songwriter and performer but as a poet, was really a vulnerable, child-like sensitive of endless curiosity. And for me, he was defined preeminently by his insatiable *curiosity*. All of his creative *expressions* of that curiosity and wonder naturally followed.

And he was apparently so vitally important to the soviet cultural appetite, that the government did little to suppress him and his recordings even though the government never officially recognized him as a singer – and, even though he often sung out against the repressive ways of his government. He'd become a household word and a cultural phenomenon in the Soviet Union, though few from the outside had ever heard of him.

Several years after getting to know him, I went to the former Soviet Union to visit him on his turf. I've never been one to stay up all night. My mental lights just turn off. Yet, staying at Vladimir's Moscow apartment, the two of us would remain talking at his kitchen table until the sun would come up. He spoke of the richness that was the Russian spirit. How the Soviet citizenry did so much with so little, and why couldn't the Soviets have more of what the Americans took for granted. We'd cry and rage. We'd laugh until we couldn't laugh anymore. This was a man so in love with every single person that lived in the Soviet Union, I could feel it rising out of his pores. His unbridled affection for his people and his resolve to be their voice, percolated up from a deep place within and burned in his heart. True to form, that passionate brush fire would take his life.

Having not spoken to Richard in nearly 30 years, I recently emailed him about Vysotsky and he wrote:

> *"Vysotsky's songs contributed to the eventual fall of the Soviet Union and its empire. He was an undeclared dissident with an exceptionally strong voice."*

---

[4] Yuri Lyubimov opened a production featuring Vladimir Vysotsky as Hamlet in 1971, at Moscow's Taganka Repertory Theater in Moscow and that production ran until Vladimir's untimely death in 1980 (217 performances in all)

Yet, not unlike many other extremely successful people I would meet in my lifetime, Volodya had kept alive within himself an active sense of wonder. And wonder wasn't something confined only to wondrous events, people and places. No. It was something that could be found anywhere and in anything. And this is *just* as a child finds wonder. The child finds wonder in, what would otherwise be considered from the adult perspective: the mundane.

Yes. Young children and the truly creative ones can wheedle wonder out of the ordinary. For me, this is the mark of true genius.

Menton, France

CHAPTER 12

Bars, Lounges and Clubs

"WHENEVER YOU'RE ASKED to sing, you sing," Volodya said with utmost seriousness. "No matter where you are or how you feel, you sing when people want you to sing," he continued. "Even when you're not asked: sing. Never hide." He would look at me with an intense seriousness and grip my forearm for emphasis.

I took Yvette to the airport to put her on a plane back to Nice. Driving home on the freeway, afterward, I howled like a wounded animal. Primitive gut-wrenching sounds that I'd never heard before made their way up from my solar plexus as I writhed in pain barely able to see the freeway ahead. It was as if a knife were twisting in my gut. No woman had ever loved me like that. And I had never loved that strongly before either. She answered some ancient longing I'd had to be cared for, mothered and loved. And her love was so deep. And I am convinced, now, that nothing is more powerful than a woman's love. I was 27 years old, restless and not wise enough to appreciate love when I saw it – and, recklessly, I let her go.

When I was 30, shortly after giving up my textile business, I rented out my house in Los Angeles for 2 years and moved to London to push my music career.

Volodya died that summer of 1980 of apparent heart failure. Over a million people attended his funeral at the Taganka Theatre in Moscow where I'd seen him play Hamlet. I felt strangely numbed and distant from the event itself. Death seemed such an odd thing to come between friends. It was incomprehensible at best. I would come to have many more experiences with loss. Those experiences would crack me open like nothing else could.

In London, after finding out that being a rock star was actually kind of difficult, I got a job singing in a club near Chelsea and Fulham on King's Road. It was a bitter disappointment to have not become instantly famous as my music publisher suggested I might be. But it was a great way to get my piano style and vocal ability up to speed. Making money at what I loved most, was a thrill. At first.

"I can travel the world," I thought to myself, "singing and playing piano."

Weeks turned to months and after playing for nearly 2 years in London and Berlin, I was ready to return home. For someone used to arising around 5am every day, the late night playing was at times a cruel mistreatment of the body...particularly the 11pm-5am schedule in Berlin 6 nights a week. It nearly did me in. The thousand-yard stare became a permanent fixture on my face as the body, deprived of sleep, floated in a surreal version of reality. Women, however, seemed available at that time and I found shelter in them to soften a growing and nagging loneliness.

Once back in Los Angeles, I found myself doing more of the same piano bar work as the rock star dream faded with the smoggy orange sunset over Will Rogers State Beach. But, this time, I sang largely in hotel lounges. The lonely hearts piled in. Everyone looking for a friend. Everyone had a story to tell. Life had dealt them a bad hand. It didn't turn out the way they'd planned. Interestingly, I've never met a person to this day whose life turned out the way they thought it would.

"My wife ran off with all my money."

"My husband was abusive."

"My husband hasn't touched me in years. I feel so frustrated."

"My business failed, and I lost everything."

"I will never trust another person for as long as I live."

The cocktail lounge, for me, was a half-way house for dramas of every size, shape and color. And on my break, I'd hear them all. Alcohol was the tell-all potion that invited people to pour out their guts and recount their stories. The stories intersected and cascaded over one another like a tapestry of the human condition. So many of them felt they were a victim. No one could have ever guessed that their life could end up this way. Everyone believing that what had happened to them was not only devastating, but insurmountable. It was the story of their lives. Life was this wily thing that happens to us and sours us on everything. And only the rich and famous are happy as well as the young and beautiful. Because they have all the money, sex and power they want. But we, the serfs, are handed the crumbs. We are victims of a rigged game.

If only. If only. If only.

I'd watch as the alcohol would dull the pain of the disappointments and loneliness. Eyes would seem to swim in their sockets as a soft translucent glaze draped over them. It was a bitterly sad environment in a lot of ways. If they didn't let on to having a lonely and disillusioned life fraught with sadness, peeling away another layer would often expose a soft and wounded underbelly. For me it was like being the hair-dresser in whom everyone entrusts all the local gossip, or the therapist that has to 'hold' all this private information from dozens of people in a small community. The job description for happy hour piano/vocalist should have included:

> You will willingly listen to the problems of others and be actively interested in helping them as they sound out every misfortune that has befallen them during the course of their desolate lives of quiet desperation. Your four hour cocktail hour stint will, therefore, include 15 minutes of client-listening and 45 minutes of playing songs that everyone knows: Songs that most can sing along to. Songs that will make people feel better. These songs will be the backdrop to this wonderful establishment where no one needs to feel alone. You, along with the drinks from the bar, are the social lubricant. You play music to help everyone forget. Yes, you. You are the music man.

I sang the songs for cocktail hour that everyone knew for several years at Sheraton Hotels, Hyatt Hotels, and Hiltons until a defining moment:

A 40-ish woman leaned bemusedly toward me over the grand piano at the Sheraton Hotel in Santa Monica -- a bra strap carelessly drooping below her shoulder. Even though *she* was the one drinking, to me her face seemed ghoulishly contorted like in a bad dream. As I was singing from behind the piano, she stared at me as she tried steadying herself weaving in an alcoholic semi-consciousness. Trying to stay composed as best I could while she leaned closer and closer to me over the top of the piano, she stuffed handful after handful of bar-peanuts in her mouth. She sputtered, "You have a pockmark on your face." With that, she exploded in laughter as I was showered in masticated peanuts.

Sometimes we just know when we're done. And I knew I was done.

I was done with the stupefyingly sad stories of the lost and the lonely. I was done with the nights of working in a dimly lit room: the drinking, the smoking and the tireless and all pervasive victim mentality. And on some level, I knew that I had my own stories of being victimized by life. I knew that I had regrets. I knew I had losses that hadn't yet found their expression in grief. I knew, that in some way, I might have even been like them.

What had happened in my life? It wasn't at all what I'd planned. I'd expected to have been married with children curled in front of the glow of a fireplace with a book. Instead I had relationships with women that rarely lasted more than 6 months. No, it was not acceptable. Although I wasn't drinking or drugging my sadness into a stupor, I was indulging in various other mind and emotion-numbing activities that relegated me, too, to the rank and file of the lost and lonely. I was really like all of them. I saw myself as a victim of "The Things that Happen in Life".

Children playing in Bali - 2011

CHAPTER 13

The Child

IT WAS ONE of the happiest days of my life when I decided that I was making enough money, doing commercial and animation voice-overs in Los Angeles, to kiss the cocktail hour and late night restaurant piano playing goodbye.

And, a few years later, another happiest day of my life was when I decided to mortgage my house and start writing and recording music for children. I wouldn't have to drive across Los Angeles in snarled traffic to do another voice-over audition, if I didn't want to. On my early morning jogs, I'd find myself crying for pure joy that I'd found something that fed me so completely. Something, that seemed so sweetly in keeping with that which I could morally justify to myself.

Several of the recordings that I did involved interviewing children with an audio field recorder. A light turned on for me. I was experiencing my own childhood through these children.

All of them little Einsteins and Vladimirs.

All of them simple, passionate, *curious*, spontaneous and funny.

What was it that they had? What did they have that the cocktail crowd had lost? They weren't victims of life. They weren't drowning in broken dreams.

What did they have that *I'd* lost? And how on earth could I get it back? I wanted the lightness that they had. To know, simply, that I'd lost something wasn't good enough. I wanted to know the steps I could take to get it back.

The children's music writing and producing became my first real first step toward the childlike qualities that I admired so much. It was a chance to sum up all I'd lost. I removed myself from the perfunctory and predictable world of the adult and began immersing myself in the world of the child.

So swept up in the child's world was I, that the direction of my life began changing before my eyes. Was this the result of the prophetic dream of collecting babies when I was 4 years old? Was I collecting the fragments of my own childhood and carefully placing them in the pram of my awareness? These children were:

> **Passionate** in a way that I wasn't.

> **Clear-thinking**, in a way I was unable to be.

> **Creative** in a way that I envied.

> **Open,** in a way that invited freshness to their perspectives which I admired.

> **Innocent,** in a way that was arresting and wise.

Innocence seemed to open the world of all possibility.

What was more, their ideas were unsullied by any kind of agenda that an adult might, otherwise, have given a corporate or political bias. Their musings were honest and uncensored. Their ideas seemed devoid of any concern for whether their musings were socially acceptable or not. The elegant simplicity and lucidity of their thoughts and imaginings stunned me and often brought me to tears.

The release of a children's CD about the environment brought me several opportunities including hosting childrens' TV shows and touring to different American cities. Touring throughout the US, I spoke mainly in elementary school assemblies. And though, outwardly, I billed myself as an environmental speaker, the gist of my talks was about encouraging children to realize and appreciate their unlimited genius as children and to use their wild and out-of-the-box creativity to heal a world bent on destroying itself. I sang the songs from the environmental CD, as I'd play a synthesizer on stage and told stories incorporating voices they'd recognized from Saturday morning cartoons I'd done.

Often the elementary schools, and occasional middle schools, were so large that the assemblies needed to be split into Kindergarten though 2nd grade and 3rd though 5th grade. As one might guess, there was a huge difference in behavior, receptivity and responsiveness in the younger groups versus the older groups. It was remarkable when I would ask, at each Kindergarten through 2nd grade assembly:

"How many dancers do we have here, today?"

The hands shot up and waved like flowers frantically bobbing about in a windy field. Their mouths were clamped shut so as not to emit an uncontrolled yell (they'd be threatened with dismissal from the assembly if they yelled out of turn.) The burst of collective energy would be evident in not only the urgently waving hands, but the jiggling of feet and the bouncing on their seats.

"How many singers?"

The hands bolted upward. Princesses? – Princes? – Actors? – Music composers? – Novelists? – Frogs? – Paper clips? : all hands went up. The energy was always electrifying.

In grades 3-5, however, the singular question: How many dancers do we have here today, resulted in the near uniformly and predictable response:

None.

If there was a tentative hand inching upwards, it was quickly silenced by the glare of other kids.

What happened?

What happens in the impossibly short time between the 2nd and 3rd grade?

I even remembered it myself. When I was a child, it was like a phantom that swept over us in the summer between the 4th and 5th grades (conformity's dust cloud didn't swoop over us *quite* as soon back then). It settled and hid in the swimming pools. Hovered over the sand at the beach. It wafted between the hot dogs sizzling on the barbeque and the picnic tables. Like a mirage rippling in the hot and dry air, it drifted up from the asphalt in front of our tract homes. We dared not stick out. We dared not be different.

Personally, I don't think we knew how to be at all. So we held back the giggles, the unguarded laughter, and the wildness and *play*fulness.

Was this the period in our lives when our socialization included messages that precluded us from being the wondrous and imaginative child we knew ourselves to be? What were the subtle, or not-so-subtle, messages codified in our socialization, anyway? What were those messages? Did they come from our friends, our parents, the radio, the magazines? It has been a question I've asked myself ever since. There must be something in it for us to not stick out. And we policed each other. We policed each other so none of us would be different and stick out! What the hell is that?

With the brilliant observations that children offered in the interviews I did with them; with the bantering back and forth during environmental-music concerts – I was book-marking all I'd lost: All that was truly sacred to me in my life.

In other adults, that loss was evident in the dreamy, faraway looks that would wash over their faces while listening to opera or classical music: The gentle swaying of the head as they'd direct an imaginary orchestra with the 'conductor's baton' that was their index finger. With eyes shut and transported far away, they were gone from the world of man. I noticed that most all adults engaged in some kind of activity to help them forget socialization's vice grip stranglehold. It has become horribly demanding to just have an ordinary life: to be responsible and do things the right way. It's as if we had all conscripted to an odious and invisible slavery that kept us off balance – never making quite enough money and never getting quite enough done. Alcohol or drugs move in to soften survival's demands on us. Or, an activity that helps us forget that we're on a treadmill: Extreme sports. Love-making. Television. Movies. Shopping. Being endlessly *busy*. We look for anything that will give us a respite from the crack of the self-imposed whip.

Children were, unwittingly, offering up the fragmented remains of my childhood that had slipped by me without notice. And that's what made them so delightful to be around. All the dreams, from my foggy youth of long ago, came rushing back. All the imaginative musings took flight once again as I temporarily shed the weighty ballast of adult responsibilities. Children kept me in touch with the few lingering aspects of my own innocence still hiding in the shadows of what had come to be my busy, busy life. Busy, busy? Yes. Because I had constructed it that way. I had constructed it that way so I wouldn't have to think about or feel the loss of all that I'd willingly given away. Next to the child's world, the busy-ness seemed like a silliness and an awful waste of one's time and energy. I vastly preferred the world of the child: The laugh that was always at the ready. The wide-eyed inquisitiveness. The fascination with all that was new. The world of strung-together marvels.

Yet, something in the environmental CD interviews blind-sided me. I asked well over a thousand children what their thoughts were about our environment:

The trees.

The air.

The oceans.

The plants.

The animals.

What I expected and what I got were often two different things. The responses were passionate, colorful and at times even dramatic. I conducted the interviews with the objectivity and impartiality of a scientist. Yet, there was something plaintive in the way they'd implore *me* to get *their* message out. There was this underlying feeling from children that adults had gone to sleep and various aspects of nature were suffering because of it. And could I please speak to the people in charge, on their behalf, about the world that they were about to inherit. I was assailed by their nervousness about the future. I was stunned by their having felt betrayed by adults. Make that: *All adults everywhere.*

These interviews were done in 1988/89 -- well before words like "sustainable" and "recycling" had made their way into common usage.

In the concert tours that followed the environmental CD, I'd urge children to not regard themselves as powerless and ineffective. I urged them to not consider themselves to be a part of the 'seen-but-not-heard' generation. Instead I asked that they view themselves as passionate little dynamos and that they had the same rights as any adult to a clean environment. And they had the right to announce their thoughts about their environment through letters to representatives and local polluting factory owners and even to the president. In the wake of the concert tours, I'd get copies of letters sent to the president; to factory owners and to councilmen with the signatures of every student of that school.

I wanted children not to accept the teachings *we* got about being seen but not heard. I wanted them to lay claim to their rightful place on this planet and be *seen* in a big way and *heard* loud and clear.

It was time to rewrite the Dr. Benjamin Spock version of child-rearing.

Without a rite of passage from childhood to adulthood, the poisoned messages of my youth persisted into adulthood such that my mere existence was apologetic. I was convinced that out of social courtesy or whatever insane and perverted notion about being the perfect child, that I should not draw attention to myself. That I had no right to be seen. I had no right to stand up for myself. I had no right to protect myself.

The hidden gift for me in helping to empower children, was that I was now helping to empower myself. I felt myself fast becoming a part of a family of children. And irrespective of the age group, I spoke to them just as I'd speak with adults...keeping all the 'big' words in the sentences and according them the same matter-of-fact respect that I'd accord an adult friend. And I sensed that they liked that. I know that kids must abhor being baby-talked to. When they're treated with respect that unceremoniously invites them into a world of equals, they very naturally step into that world.

After the environmental CD, I wrote a lullaby album. Before recording one of the songs, I got my mother on the phone and played it for her.

> "How'd you know how to compose a lullaby for children if you've never had a child?" my mother asked.

> "I just pretended that I had a child and I was singing to it," I said not realizing what I was really saying.

> "I don't get it," she said, "you must be some actor, because that song sounds like you really have a baby."

And what I realized was, I composed and sang the songs that I wanted to have sung to me. And in whatever effort to self-soothe or re-parent myself, I sang to a place deep inside that simply never got what it wanted. That's when an important light turned on.

Maya on our wedding day - 1994

CHAPTER 14

Of Gains and Losses & Resurrection

THERE WAS SOMETHING emerging within me. Awakening to the child energy around me coaxed sense memories, long-forgotten musings and dreams to the surface again. I thought that slowing down and moving to Oregon would would be a good thing. It was to take stock of all that I'd lost. It was a concerted effort to simplify to a rural lifestyle knowing I would be no longer able to do voice overs or music performance. And then, the 'things that happen in life' – happened to me.

Three years into living in Ashland, I'd met, married and lost my wife to a fatal car crash. All in the same year. 1994. The unspeakable sadness, trauma and sense of the surreal put me in touch with moments reminiscent of the nervous breakdown 34 years earlier. I quite suddenly found myself in a world that had nothing to do with the reality everyone else was participating in. My normal filtering systems had been disabled and I was living with a nakedly raw and sensitive awareness that was operating without any social conditioning or preconceptions.

This was the purest of pure states:

Pure pain.

Pure vertigo.

Pure sadness.

Pure hell.

And whatever was remaining of a self concept had been, purely, stripped away.

I was vulnerable. Shattered. Adrift. Bereft.

My life had been razed as if by an ice field sweeping across every corner of my life. The erasure of all familiar comforts was complete, leaving behind a desert-like absence and an aching heart. A veil slid over my eyes covering whatever remaining light there was. My child. My adult. My countrified life-style. Gone.

There was only the barren moment. And the moment was, at times, unbearable. I'd come to a complete dead end in the road and all the sadness and grief of a lifetime trailed behind the one consuming loss – the loss of my wife. I couldn't run or get busy this time. I could only stare blankly into this whirlpool of feelings.

I limped along for the next 10 years or so trying to scrape together the remnants of a life lost. Dreams lost. Until I decided that instead of scraping together the shard remains of the past, I'd script something for myself exactly as I saw fit.

Throwing myself into swing-dancing lessons and re-entering my involvement with children lifted the spirits considerably. They both helped me to feel lighter and more in touch with an essential, but often ignored, part of myself.

Between putting together production projects to live off of, I interviewed children and teenagers this time from around the world. One project was called A Kid's EyeView and its companion series: A Teen's EyeView. But different from the audio CD this was for a TV pilot I was working on. I made time to travel. I used what little funds I had to go to places around the globe I'd never been to. And travel was my old friend. It was like music to be able to hear different languages singing in my ears. Every language its own song. The song of a culture. The song of a societal belief set. The song of countless joys, sorrows and the rhythms of life. And the children's voices, though inflecting their respective languages and cadences differently, were all saying essentially the same things:

I want to be happy, but things can all seem so complicated.

And, once again, a theme recurrent in the interviews I had done on the earlier audio CD, ten or so years earlier, was appearing once again:

> How could adults have allowed things to get so out of control. In short:

> How could adults, in good conscience, hand a world over to their children that is basically the remains of a lifestyle of irresponsible over consumption?

And, really, that was my question too. What part of our adult sensibilities had we taken leave of to ask our children and young adults to clean up *our* mess, when I thought we were the evolved generation? Or perhaps more accurately, what part of us did not feel we were even *leaving* a mess behind for them to sort out? We were the ones that called attention to the atrocities of the Vietnam war. We were the ones calling many of the corporate agendas amoral and sometimes nefarious. We were the ones asking for social justice and equality. We were the ones asking that we slow down and appreciate the miracle of life. We were vocal, involved and proactive. But, presumably, once caught up in fending for our own financial survival, we forgot about our ideals. We forgot about the urgency to get world governments to pay more attention to programs that actually benefit people instead of extinguishing them. And when we weren't looking, we became the 'suits'. We became the 'man'. We handed off a world, caving in on itself, to the very children we told bedtime stories to; sang to; and told them we loved them. Night after night.

"Good night. I love you. Don't let the bedbugs bite."

Nura

CHAPTER 15

Innocence is a Muscle

"Children are the purest of all of us. They have the clearest of ideas.

...All adults, when they were children, were innocent. All of them...but somewhere along the way, with everything that happens, they change.

...It's like when you exercise. If you don't exercise (your innocence), you lose it."

---Nura - age 14, Colonia, Uruguay (November, 2008)

REALIZING SHE MIGHT have already lost something, a melancholy swept across her face. She was sensing the slipping away of her own innocence. And, as is often the case with others I've interviewed, she was forming opinions about who she'd become in real time. The interview gave her the chance to actually articulate what she'd been ruminating over for some time. Two key elements for me in what she said were:

"...but somewhere along the way, with everything that happens, they (adults) change."

She was fully aware that there are *things that happen in life.* And these things tend to take away something precious and irreplaceable.

"...if you don't exercise (your innocence) you lose it."

When she said these words, I was struck by the simplicity and forthrightness of the conviction. I thought it was absolutely brilliant that she saw that the loss of innocence wasn't a cultural inevitability, rather that it was something we could actually choose to keep. That it's we who are in control here. And, that we are not the hapless victims of life's circumstances. We are not victimized by our culture, our failed relationships, the banks, our policy-makers or anything else.

Before interviewing her, Nura didn't know what kinds of questions I'd ask. I'd gotten the interview through a friend of a friend while in Uruguay. I'd told, the fourteen-year-old, I was working on a pilot for a TV program and was interviewing children and young adults from around the world about their environment and their hopes and dreams for the future. After the first few questions about environmental activism and Nura's friends at school, we found ourselves unexpectedly talking about lost innocence. She wondered if it might be her fate, too.

I had seen this several times before. Also, once in Marseille, while interviewing Latifa, a 17 year old French Muslim woman, she got swept up in the emotion of what the human race had become as a global community: Everyone fending for themselves. Governments behaving in greedy self-interest while not having the least bit of interest in the very public that supports them.

Latifa heard herself say that the world needed a prophet or savior to get the people back on track. She felt that the people needed to be intervened on by something from the outside: Something outside of the narrow periphery of the human perspective. Something divine. She looked away as tears welled in her eyes.

While the questions I asked kids were confined to the health of our national environment like on the children's CD[1] from years before, I began venturing questions to teenagers for The Teens EyeView Series like:

What would an ideal world look like?

---

[1] *A Kid's Eye View of the Environment.* CD released in 1989 MichaelMishMusic ASCAP

What would it actually take to create that ideal world?

What is it about our human nature that would allow for war to exist?

What makes you truly and wonderfully happy?

Different from the nature themed CDs, the EyeView Series[2] involved camera interviews of children and teens from different countries around the world. And while doing those interviews, something presented itself with undeniable clarity:

> Children and teens have a far greater facility at providing solutions to our planet's social, environmental and political problems than adults. And further, they have a clearer understanding as to where and how adults went wrong. The irony in all this is that we think *we* teach *them* when in fact my experience has shown that if we remove ourselves from the role of parent or teacher, we have one hell of a lot more to learn from them. The twist in all this, of course, is that children inescapably become adults themselves.

Irrespective, however, of how ever many aspects of a child's innocence are stripped from them by the time they're 8 or so, often one element of innocence remains. Passion. Children and adolescents seem tirelessly passionate about everything in their worlds. Passion is the engine of change. Passion is what fuels the flower to follow the sun in its transit across the sky. Passion creates magic. Passion makes life more alive.

If what Nura said was true:

> "...but somewhere along the way, with everything that happens, they (adults) change."

How could I find out *what*, exactly, happens and why?

---

[2] *A Kid's Eye View* and *A Teen's Eye View* – www.aKidsEyeView.com

Saint Aubin, Switzerland - 2011

CHAPTER 16

Why the Background?

WHILE MY EARLY years were decidedly different than yours, the results can often be counted on as being the same. Things happened in our lives that changed us. No matter how functional our family lives were, most of us in the West lose something vital along the way. Unless, as Nura says, we exercise our innocence, something precious is no longer part of us by the time we're officially socialized. What's worse is: We willingly give it away for the door prize:

The reward for doing everything 'right'.

And in my life, for example, no one was to blame for this. Not my parents. Not society (whatever *that* is). Not the American, or any other, culture. It's, quite simply, one of those things that *happens*. On some broad level I chose to be stripped of my innocence. I chose to give it away to the highest bidder: The Western God of conformity. And the God of conformity was everywhere. It was in school. It was in magazines. It was on the radio and, in the 60's, it was just getting its legs on TV. It was in my neighborhood. It was in my house. It was even within the sweet promise of the first kiss. It was the great ubiquity in my upbringing as it remains to be to this day. And it knocks ever more insistently at the door. But in retrospect, I can see that innocence's erosion, was both systematic and unavoidable. Discipline and conformity erode spontaneity and innocence. Peer pressure contributes to the stripping away of innocence. After all, where is the *reward* for behaving innocently? In the adult world innocence means weakness and weakness means we're eaten up in a competitive culture. And to be eaten up in a collective that is competition-based means social death.

Discouraging the active imagination whose seed can only sprout from innocence, seems an essential ingredient to the successful functioning of a society in the Western world. The imaginative ones are discouraged from their imaginings. What is more, they have no place in a world of machine men with machine minds.

But I am not living for my culture. I respect it and it has to be admired. But the culture must end where my psyche begins.

The real question, and it's been a lifelong question:

Can I have passion, wonder, vitality and curiosity revitalized in my life again?

We see innocence and it melts our hearts. And innocence remains everywhere in nature.

I can watch kittens or puppies cavorting for hours and never be bored or unamused...not for a second. From tree squirrels to dolphins, everyone seems to be having the times of their lives...except us.

There have been those wonderful moments in my life where wonder has erupted like a geyser. I've played endlessly with dolphins in the wild. And no experience quite compares to those glorious times interacting with dolphins. Like the Balinese, they look for ways to play. They express themselves in the only way any life is ever meant to express itself:

In celebration.

Celebration is the only appropriate response to the gift of life.

And, though it sounds like I'm anthropomorphizing here and I'm quite sure I'm not, they *look for reasons to laugh*. Dolphins love to laugh. Anyone who has ever played with a dolphin in the wild knows they love to laugh.

Tree squirrels, too. I've played hide and seek with them. Nothing is more satisfying to the soul than playing hide and seek with another species. Yet, we have no time for play. Certainly not like animals do. Why?

We have to make a living. And making a living seems to create stress.

We have to wear a social face when working with our colleagues.

We have to make enough money to pay bills 'just to survive'.

We have to work at being in a relationship.

We have to work.

Sure. We get to play. On weekends maybe; Memorial and Labor Day weekends; Christmas, and after we retire. What a life! What happened? And has it always been like this?

Can I get back to innocence? Can *we*?

My best guess?:

Yes.

TABLE OF CONTENTS

The Reclaiming of Innocence

PART 2

CHAPTER 17

Acculturation, Trauma, Unexamined Grief, and Stress

A "loss of innocence" is a common theme in fiction and pop culture, and is often seen as an integral part of coming of age. It is usually thought of as an experience or period in a child's life that widens their awareness of evil, pain or suffering in the world around them.

-Wikipedia

How did *I* lose it???

How do any of us lose it?

I looked at my own life as an example:

- The birth trauma

- The hyper-vigilance, motivated by staying safe and being lovable

- The trauma of being burnt as a 4-year-old signaled to me that everything could change for the worse at a moments notice

- The *perception* of being abandoned at having to go to school

- The rules and disciplines

- The first heart break

- The need for acceptance by a peer group

- The pursuit of love and the acquisition of things to reduce a sense of loneliness

- The stress related to making money

- The little and big losses

I examined the aspects of my life that contributed most prominently to the stealthy erasure of my childhood innocence.

But I would be kidding myself if I didn't start from the very beginning: the trauma of birth.

Like most of us, I was brought into this world with a deficit. Jean Liedloff would say:

> "The two words that I've arrived at to describe what we all need to feel about ourselves, children and adults, in order to perceive ourselves accurately, are *worthy* and *welcome*. If you don't feel worthy and welcome, you really won't know what to do with yourself. You won't know how to behave in a world of other people. You won't think you deserve to get what you need."[1]

War is waged on us from the time we come out of the womb. In most of our cases, we moved from warm and cozy to cold, uncomfortable and, at times, downright hostile. By the time I was placed on my mother's chest after being spanked, weighed, measured, swabbed, poked, sprayed, and circumcised, much of the damage had been done. Pretty much, from that moment

---

[1] An Interview with Jean Liedloff by Chris Mercogliano. Jean Liedloff is author of the *Continuum Concept*

forward, life was starting to look like a big fat drag because something was terribly wrong and I hadn't the remotest idea what it was.

Non-traumatized babies, who are conceived and born in love, display an amazing degree of intelligence, kindness, common sense and good health. They are good communicators, peaceful, attentive, caring, alert, self-motivated human beings, free from aggressive, self-destructive addictions.

Natural birth does require some preparation these days, for the art of birthing has been almost lost. In tribal life it was supposed to be a mother's gift to her daughter, a natural obvious transmission. But with the modern day stress level and easy access to drugs, in the US, for example, 95% of births are considered traumatic. 50% rated as moderate trauma, 45% of them are rated as 'severely traumatic'.

© 2011 Elena Vladimorova BirthIntoBeing.com

The nights following my birth only underscored the original terror.

Every frighteningly lonely night, isolated in a crib, was war: My plea to be held in arms versus my parents' will to get me over the crying hump to keep me from being a demanding devil-child. The more I cried, the greater my parent's resolve to 'break' my need for attention. Whether it was Benjamin Spock's writing itself or the ways in which we chose to interpret Dr. Spock's books, there were several generations of emotional casualties inflicted on the infants of this planet. And my parents did everything right: They did everything by the book like all parents of that generation.

I cried by way of saying 'I'm not comfortable sleeping alone because I'm a defenseless baby. Would someone please let me know I'll be ok?' My parents let me cry it out by way of saying 'This is breaking our heart, but this is something you're going to have to get used to because certain things in life are tough and this is one of them. Otherwise, we'll be responsible for having spoiled you, and your whole miserable life will be our fault.' And why would my parents do it any differently than that which was done with them? And how could they have known? They were simply doing all the 'right things' as the conventional wisdom of the time would have them do. But how many of us have simply stopped to look at our prescription for raising a baby? We've handed down this 'breaking in' period as if it's necessary and it's our obligation as parents. I remember when we closed the bathroom door on our new puppy to be left in there on a wad of blankets at night until he got over his need to be with the rest of the 'pack'. We'd solemnly agree we 'had' to do it even though our hearts were breaking at the woeful puppy howls all night long. We'd agreed, without checking with our hearts, that there is a crying out period for puppies and babies. It was like a passage. And, where this got started, it boggles the mind. I can only guess that the inferiority complexes we came in with decided us to put the advice of 'experts' above the authority of our own feelings.

So exhausted and defeated, was I, in this showdown of wills that my brain went to the one place a brain could go: something is very wrong and I must have done something to make it that way. So, it only followed that without an inner sense of rightness, any disturbance or disquietude that reinforced the feeling that something was wrong, would inevitability cement itself in my psyche. Disturbances like:

I'm not lovable.

My misery must be because I did something bad.

There's something wrong.

I'm nervous and don't know why.

The primitive limbic, or emotional, brain simply stores the birth and infancy experience as a largely disruptive succession of events and hands off the rest of the brain's development to the cerebral cortex.

"Alright, I've done all I can do here. Over to you, cerebral cortex. Oh, and CC? Good luck. See you in 60 years or so when you try to make sense of all this. Until then, I'll be hiding."

It's like the primitive limbic brain is our operating system and the rest of the left brain is our data drive as it collects and stores information. If this is even anywhere close to an accurate metaphor, it's not hard to see how the idea of being born into sin has had such an enduring hold in Western religious belief: because the operating system is carrying on behind the scenes. And all the data is experienced with the skewed underlay of an operating system suggesting something is simply not right.

>The sky is blue (but something's not right).

>This glade is beautiful (but something's not right).

>I feel like I have so much love to give (but something's not right).

>Does a day get better than this? (but what's wrong?)

I'd proffer that the Western birth trauma and the subsequent crying-it-out period characterized by not being held in arms, is the firmament upon which all psychic disturbances spring. That said, what kinds of beliefs and experiences were able to sprout from my 'something's not right' soil?:

The 4 Innocence Eaters and their Cousins

Acculturation, Trauma, Unexamined Grief and Stress

These four, more than most other life events I know of, caused me to choose to walk away from innocence. And, again, they are branches off the "something's not quite right, here" tree – or, the symptoms of an errant and defective operating system.

Acculturation

Acculturation happens when we are made aware of the rules of the culture: The rules that constitute the societal "norm". We sign on to the norm, and are accepted. We don't sign on, and we're not accepted. It's probably just that simple. And for me, the pressure to be accepted was so very strong it felt like it was a matter of life and death. I'd go so far as to say that much of the attention and energy spent all of my life has been around the concern of what others thought about me. Will my thoughts, actions and, virtually my presence in the world, be seen as 'normal and acceptable'? Being accepted comes with such rich rewards that it's virtually impossible not to go that route unless we are raised with an extremely secure sense of self...and a sense of rightness in that self.

I've long felt that we are eased into our culture, initially, in the womb with the soft musical strains of the mother's voice as she gently imparts to us the ways of the culture. The visceral understanding of the culture into which we are born is understood, prenatally I believe, in the melodic and codified cadences of the mother's voice. She speaks during the course of a day and, as a fetus, we hear only the melody of her voice: The tonal rising and falling of her speech. Our first experience with social programming, then, is within that melody which has the ancestral legacy imprint as well as the mother's own life experience written into it. We come into the world strongly predisposed to generations of cultural stories that we glean, prenatally in this supremely empathetic state, from the song of the mother. It's reintroduced in the home and underscored during our education which dually serves to categorize and define the aspects of our culture and to socialize us.

For years, I had a body-work practice where I would help to deconstruct limiting beliefs that my clients had. And, because most of those beliefs seemed to be integrated into the body at a time when my client was precognitive, I set upon undoing the beliefs in the same way that they were embedded in the body awareness originally: with sound. With softly vibrating transducers under a heated water bed and headphones fit snugly to their ears, the client was coaxed with imagery into a deeply relaxed state. I addressed the cells of the body directly...just as they had received the information, themselves, prenatally. With the recorded sounds of the ocean, sine waves from a frequency generator, gentle music and the sound of my voice being deliberately vibrated into their body from the transducers under the waterbed, the newly imparted information replaced the limiting belief information (ideally). Maybe none of it worked. Maybe it did. But just being in a relaxed state and hearing positive messages could have been as important as anything else. As with most of us, my clients lived inside their beliefs about themselves. We can't name something that is going on in our awareness using the same busy tabulating brain that certainly placed it all there in the first place. Using Hakomi and simply observing my client's body movements, I could sense what their limiting beliefs were. This isn't some talent I happen to have...we all do it, on some level, with each other.

It would be great if we could simply reflect our observations back to our friends avoiding the temptation to either therapize or criticize them. We can do so much for one another (but, this is another chapter or another book).

Once we are children, suggestions about how we are limited come barreling toward us at super sonic speed. If we had a sense of being "worthy and welcome", those suggestions couldn't 'dock' in our belief set. Instead:

> As soon as an adult tells a child that the grass he is painting in his picture should be green and not blue...

> As soon as a child is told she shouldn't sing because it doesn't sound good...

> As soon as a child is told that he can't be an astronaut...

> As soon as a child is told that she lives in a dream world...

> As soon as a child is told to not play the violin because it "sounds like a cat crying"...

> As soon as a child is told to brush their hair so they can look more 'presentable'...

> As soon as we are told that fairies don't exist...

> ...the rules and admonishments of the culture slowly eclipse what ever remaining sense of rightness, worthiness and welcome we have. That sense of rightness, therefore, becomes something we aspire to and not something we already (and innately) have.

While the rules are good for an efficiently operating culture, it can be completely ruinous to the child's sense of play, creativity, imagination and his innocence.

> Phrases that would haunt me as a kid:

> Stop imagining things.

> Don't let your imagination run away with you.

> What are you imagining now?

> Oh come on. It's all in your imagination.

> Stop your dreaming!

What is with us anyway? Do teachers, parents and peers not see that if it wasn't for the imaginative ones and day dreamers and those that don't follow all the rules, there would *be* no cars; there would *be* no bicycles or scientific theories. No sewing machines, pick axes or blenders? Everything that we appreciate about our modern conveniences, we owe to the dreamers. From primitive man's first discovery of fire to our present-day ability to hurl through our upper atmosphere in a jet. These are things we take for granted and don't even wonder how they work. How on earth did the transistor radio armed with nothing more than a solitary battery, inside it, spring to life and allow me to hear muffled songs long after 'lights out' through my pillow?! Some dreamer thought this up. And that dreamer was fixedly in that innocent and childlike place of: The world of all possibility.

He was a dreamer.

Not the student voted most likely to succeed.

Not the valedictorian.

She was the one staring out the window imagining a hundred better places to be.

Now, as I write in the area of Switzerland where I spent 5 months wrestling with my sanity when I was 20 years old, I remember the words said more than any others at the family dinner table where I stayed:

"...comme il faut" (...like you're supposed to)

Behave like you're supposed to. Eat properly. Study like you're supposed to.

As well as:

"Ca ne va pas, ou bien?" (Is there something wrong with you?)

These were the post hypnotic suggestions to keep everyone in the family safe. These were the reminders to keep the members of the family within conformity's cushioned inner sanctum.

The insistence that there is only one correct way to do things is an ever-present reinforcement of a cultural/social order. And that social order only tolerates certain behaviors that are deemed acceptable. To choose to be outside of social acceptability, is a dark and lonely path, or so we seem convinced. I think we even think it's dangerous.

Hearing the "comme il faut" again sends my memory careening back to all those sense impressions I had when I was 20 years old and working in a factory, here. The "comme il faut"'s dropped all around me with the constant reminder of the singular way to 'do' a given thing:

The right way.

And I figure it's no coincidence that I chose Switzerland as a place to finish the writing of this book. Nowhere in my experience are social conventions adhered to more ardently than in Switzerland. It's a country that prides itself in being ordered and on-time. Defined and precise. For a good many things, Switzerland is a fantastic place to be because one can always *count* on things being a certain way and a predictable way. So, in that respect, the Swiss have written the book on how to live in the left hemisphere of the brain. Things are correct. They are accounted for. They are pre-tested and predefined. And it's done to perfection in a way that can only be admired. And in so many ways Switzerland is exemplary of a social order that functions to the letter. And, over the years, it has done an amazing job at keeping itself a responsible, integrated and respected country. Geographically and politically, it seems to be a model of functional elegance and self-reliance.

The right and wrong way to do and perceive things creates its own tidy package that eliminates lots of the cultural gray area. Behaviors are checked and rechecked to make sure that all behavior fits within the description of the national and societal agreement. One has only to cross the border from Switzerland into Italy, to see just how different one cultural agreement can be to another. Of course, these cultural disparities are not quite as salient today because social structures are crumbling and, from one day to the next, countries are profiling themselves differently.

This has caused me to take a hard look at the ways in which I, too, police myself. "Would so-and-so approve of what I'm doing right now?" "Am I taking too much time off from working?" And these checks and balances are underscored by my family, my friends and, what has come to be the quintessential "decider" of what's acceptable and what is not: the behavioral norms as are exemplified through *television*. I'll leave the way television impacts us as a culture to the behaviorists. For me, TV reinforces the mores and folkways in a given society. It ultimately defines the 'goods' and the 'bads' as is decreed in the programming and is followed by the Greek Chorus of commercials between programs. Television endorses the acceptable and eschews the profane. And this is easily seen in the re-enacted life dramas on a TV series, in films and news presentations.

The way I've been socialized sits on my shoulder like a judge. And often, my creative expressions haven't always fallen within the accepted parameters of my culture. For example, some friends and family were made uncomfortable at my decision to simply travel for an indefinite amount of time.

"Don't you know where you're going?"

"When are you going to stop running?"

"I hope you find what you're looking for."

By now, after many forays of leaping headlong into the unknown, I've come to understand and, strangely, even expect these reactions. I'm always being asked what my plan is.

"What's your plan?"

"I don't have one," I often reply.

"You *have* to have a plan."

At this point in the conversation, I'll make one up just to quell the discomfort of the concerned friend or family member.

When I hitch-hiked in Europe for nearly 2 years in my early 20's, drivers would often ask:

"How long have you been traveling like this?"

"About a year or so," I'd answer.

"Really? And how much longer are you going to travel?"

"I'm not sure," I'd reply.

"Not sure, eh?" they'd say trailing off into an escapist day-dream.

Then the far-away look washed over their face. It was a far-away look that I'd continue to see many times. While the idea of it seemed frightening, they imagined themselves stepping outside the confines of their responsibilities. They imagined themselves with everything they owned perched on their back and a thumb out waiting for their next ride and their next adventure. Yes. I can spot the far-away look even to this day. Unlike the thousand yard stare that suggests that the mind is desperately trying to forget images too macabre to comprehend, the far-away look suggests that the mind is being sweetly urged to remember images of whimsy and delight too wondrous to *ever* forget.

And I'm the first to admit it: I feel far more normal, safe and credible when I'm doing everything within the cultural guidelines. I feel less lonely and less insecure. But it has become no longer a choice for me. I cannot do it anymore. I simply need to live the rest of my life on my terms and not on the terms of this societal edict suggesting that I follow the strict protocols that were drilled into me during my 12 years of public school.

How do I undo a life-long addiction to social habits? Because if innocence is what I'm looking to connect with, I do not feel it can live side-by-side in a mechanical and reality-adjusted world.

What are these social habits, anyway?

OK. I'm ashamedly habituated to keeping busy so I don't have to think or feel. I'm addicted to the feedback I get from others. I'm addicted to approval, to love, to movies, to comfort, to familiarity... I could go on. And I'm sure that I'm not alone. We're in a social agreement that keeps us on a tight leash and it doesn't come without its stressors:

> I feel like going for a long country walk, but I have to work.

> I feel like telling my boss that he shouldn't treat people that way.

> I feel like saying *exactly* what I feel.

And every time I need to swallow hard and not do what I want, it's a stress. And the stress shows up as a deepening divide between my social "I" and the "I" of my spontaneous heart. Over time, this duplicity builds up an emotional kind of scarring. A scarring that can be temporarily eased in mind numbing activities. Because were I to go into the middle of the discomfort that is created by the schism, I'd be forced to change my life. And it may be a change that is not acceptable for those to whom I'm responsible, or to those that need me to remain being the person they know me to be so they can be 'comfortable'. Once the door is opened; once the rabbit hole is entered, there's no turning back and our lives are never the same again. For most of us, changing our world-view means dying and then creating something, with no road map, from the ground up. And, once in middle age, it's easier to just plop ourselves in front of the TV and watch something on the Nature Channel.

To that end, I have been stunningly adept at being able to minimize responsibilities all of my life. This has been a vexation to many around me, particularly my family. But in the immortal words of my tell-it-like-it-is New York friend, Lyle:

"Whose life are you living, anyway...?" As simple and over-used as that question is, when Lyle asked me this question, it was like hearing it for the first time. A switch was flipped and I set out to find an honest answer.

The way we all 'check in' on each other has an amazing power over us. We stay within the social zone of safety at the risk of being unaccepted. As Marina Vlady walked me through the Moscow streets on a dark December afternoon in 1978, I asked her why everyone seemed so guarded and careful. She said that anyone at anytime could just point a finger at a person and say "you..you...YOU!". If anyone stuck out from the crowd for any reason, not the police, not government officials and not the KGB, but people..*people* in the streets could make someone a heretic, counter-revolutionary or an undesirable. THAT is the power of conformity – the possible madness within the mass consciousness. This was when Communism was still very alive in the Soviet Union and this was one of the reasons it worked so well. It worked on the: *Fear of how others would judge us.* When the mercury of fear is high on the cultural thermometer, power is an easy thing to wield over a people. It's always been that way. And, God, I wish it were not so.

As long as innocence can be kept out of the many-tentacled reach of social acceptability, innocence can thrive. That's what I feel to be true for myself. How to strike a balance between personal innocence and living in an adult world with adult rules, is a question. This is where an artful re-examination of a life-style becomes necessary.

Beliefs

Beliefs are woven into the consensus reality of a culture. The act of being socialized is the acceptance of a mountain of beliefs formed by the many people that came before us in our culture. We get thrust in this world like extra-terrestrials and we slowly adopt the cultural beliefs as our own until we feel that we've internalized them. We carefully measure them with the help of a lot of "comme il fauts'" until we've got them memorized and they are tantamount to being a part of our autonomic nervous system. When the belief set of the culture is installed, things go smoothly for us...for a while anyway. This ensures the efficient, well-oiled functionality of a social system. And while it is beneficial to an efficient social machine, it isn't necessarily beneficial for an emotionally healthy individual. Artists are the ones that help us to remember who we are irrespective our our social system. (This will be elaborated on in chapter 9.)

The moment when I was driving down the freeway after having driven my new sports car off the lot, things clicked for me. I had signed on, like an actor in a play, and I was 'happy'. I wasn't suffering with the endless solitude on the fringes of poverty and social unacceptability. I was successful in the social model I'd been plunked in the middle of, and this was the payoff: My hair dancing in the wind with the top down on my sports car as I was laughing out loud speeding in and out of traffic. I had gone from being an alien in a foreign land to being accepted. And the acceptance felt really, really...good.

For me now, any belief I have about myself, about anyone, about anything...impinges vitally on my ability to be present in the discovery and wonder zone. In the world of all-possibility, any belief is axiomatically a limiting belief. But what is beneath the matrix of my beliefs? And how on earth do I shed the influences of my culture-based beliefs to find out what is beneath them?

Undoing the social programing of the primitive or emotional brain is the most slippery of all of the things to take on. This is because the very brain I'm using to undo the effects of errant thinking and the destructive aspects of socialization, has been socialized itself: socialized with rules, beliefs, mores and social structures.

It's like a spider trying to disassemble a spider web when all the spider knows...is building them. And as we know, all the belief constructs we've learned from infancy make up the stage on which all other beliefs are played. So how do I strip away my social influences without deconstructing my stage? When my stage just happens to be who I am?

And here is the error in thinking. I am assuming that I *am* my beliefs; that I am my own socialization. And *that's* what makes it tricky and precarious terrain. I need to see social convention as an *influence* and not as a programming that I'm indefinitely stuck with.

If my astrological sign *influences* who I am, I have to remember that it does not *define* who I am. Similarly, I am influenced but not defined by my socializing determinants. So if I can step outside of 'myself' long enough to simply notice what's influencing me, I can feasibly regard acculturation as another facet of the wonder of life....like science...like math...like horses running among sand dunes. I can observe it and say, "wow, look at that!"

The question:

How do I begin noticing – without thinking *I am* what I'm noticing?

This is the most mind-numbing consideration because it is the most existential. The one noticing, is noticing that he is noticing. It's like the two mirrors facing each other at the barber shop when I was a kid. I got lost in the endless reflections and noticed just how utterly maddening the idea of infinity was. But this does not necessarily pose the quandary it might suggest.

If I can just relax (huge idea), and notice the feelings parading across the stage of my awareness without identifying with them, I think that's all there is to it. "Oooo, it's Michael pretending to be Michael with all these...these thoughts and feelings. Whoah, that's so interesting."

Trauma

Trauma can most quickly slam the door on innocence. We've all seen the, now, iconic 1985 National Geographic cover photo of the *Afghan Girl*. Her searing green eyes revealing horrors that we, in the air-conditioned comforts of our Western homes, can't even imagine.

She could have been a girl playing with her friends on the street in front of her house. In one singular and defining moment, the atomic blast of trauma like an ink blot on her life's time-line, turned her childhood into a desert and whatever playfulness that defined her youth disappeared never to return again. Wasn't that why that particular photograph had such an enduring impact on all of us? Because the eyes told us more about the atrocities of war than any reporter ever could. What is more: It spoke of the sudden loss of innocence as a result of a traumatic experience. Leaving us to imagine what that traumatic event was, only makes her image more powerful. Our imaginations can concoct scenes far more disturbing than even the most skilled of Hollywood special effects artists because we draw on our own unique set of personal emotional triggers. All of us can, on some level, relate to the *Afghan Girl* because we all have an *Afghan Girl* inside of us. We all have had a defining event that sealed our innocence from us, and in some cases forever.

Trauma comes in many forms. It is most certainly not limited to war and combat-related events. It is what we have come to call: The things that happen to us in life.

When we look at a baby, how many of us think privately: 'How long will this baby have its innocence before some occurrence rocks its world and it can no longer giggle at a colorful ball as it dances across the floor?'

I think the reason why the *Afghan Girl* had such an impact on us as an icon for the atrocities of war, was because we all see ourselves in her eyes. We've all had trauma, and if you're like me, we've had more than a few.

Some of the traumas that Wikipedia sites are:

Physical Trauma

- An often serious and body-altering physical injury, such as the removal of a limb

- Blast injury, a type of physical trauma caused by an explosion

- Blunt trauma, a type of physical trauma caused by impact or other force applied from or with a blunt object

- Penetrating trauma, a type of physical trauma in which the skin or tissues are pierced by an object

Psychological Trauma

- An emotional or psychological injury, usually resulting from an extremely stressful or life-threatening situation

It's so interesting to me that the word Traum, in German, means: dream.

For those of us that have been traumatized, the event, itself, seems dream-like and surreal. Even in an auto accident (and I hope you haven't been in one), events during the accident seem to slow way down. I have had the experience, while the accident is unfolding, of actually having the presence of mind to mentally articulate:

> Oh, that was a vicious crunching sound. That will mean I won't be using this leg for a minimum of 4 months. And *this* will mean I might be bleeding for around 45 minutes. And, I'll have to get this muscle repaired. Oh man, I wonder if they even have a surgery for this. I suppose that this popping sound means I'll have to spend the night in the hospital. Who's going to water my plants?

And these mental notes usually come from a witnessing voice within me that seems, curiously, unattached and entirely objective as the accident progresses from one injury to the next. After the traumatic event has happened, a tirelessly long process of trying to figure out what, exactly, happened inevitably follows.

If I haven't figured out what actually happened, the dream-like event persists as it imprints itself in my body and emotions.

Victims of PTSD[2] are often plagued with hellish flashbacks and nightmares or they have difficulty getting to sleep. Anger, hyper-vigilance and avoidance, as a result of and associated with the trauma, also speak to the body and mind trying to make sense of that frozen moment in time when life changed for that person.

Though not necessarily the stuff of PTSD, we have all had moments that have been traumatic. And, it could just as easily be a trauma caused by not getting to our child in time when she has had an accident. Or, even being told we have an incurable disease. There's the trauma of our partner telling us it's not working for him or her anymore. I've probably had a dozen accidents, many of them needing surgery and/or physical therapy, and I can only guess how many of those accidents still live in my body memory. Every time, for example, a car is tail-gating me, my body goes into a clench of reliving being rear-ended and the dreaded folding of metal and the following interminable visits to the chiropractor afterward. We live, not only amidst

---

[2] Post-traumatic stress disorder is a type of anxiety disorder. It can occur after you've seen or experienced a traumatic event that involved the threat of injury or death. A.D.A.M. Medical Encyclopedia

trauma, but we live with the potential for more traumatic events every day. It's the stuff that happens in life.

To unlock the grip trauma has had on me from a panoply of brushes with death and sudden shocks to the system, I have had to notice where the traumas are locked. There are, in my opinion, formidable methods of unlocking these traumas – some probably as traumatic as the event itself (like hypnosis and Rolfing etc.). But I have chosen, as with grief, to simply *notice* the tightening muscle; the shoulder tensing; the jaw tightening etc.

Can innocence live where there has been trauma and there is the likely prospect of repeated trauma. No. Not in my opinion. Not if the trauma still lives in the body and mind. In an attempt to at least relate to the stored trauma in my body, I've been known to talk the cells in my body like a friend:

> "You guys have been through it, haven't you? You know it wasn't anything you did wrong, it was just stuff that happened. Oh, and you know something else? I've really appreciated all you've done for me in the past. You guys are great. Really. You've been an immensely appreciated part of the whole two legs, two feet and torso thing. Oh, and all those organs you make work individually and together -- I'm here to congratulate you on being able to figure it all out. It's a wonder to me. You're great. Awesome, really. You just keep on giving. But, I know you're repairing yourselves right now, and I just want you to let me know if there's anything you need...or, anything I can do. Kay? You know...juicing, fasting, chocolate...name it."

Grief

Grief is gently calling us with a kind of Homerian insistence to get back home and take a closer look at what we've lost. Unexpressed grief takes its toll with its constant reminder that 'something's wrong'. The limbic brain is clear on that score. It remembers the birth trauma and the crying, at being left alone, like it was yesterday. *We* don't. But, *it* does. And because it does, it is still locked in there. It makes itself known to us on the seams of our thoughts and musings.

In my own journey through grief and assisting others through theirs, it's become so patently obvious that we all are processing grief, to a greater or lesser degree, all the time. The only difference, from person to person, is some are aware of it and others are not. I've seen it with myself: the death of my wife brought up not only the grief central to her loss, but every ungrieved death or loss experience I'd ever had. And it was then that I'd realized that grief had been just beneath my radar for quite a long time. Interestingly, I've had a bitter-sweet association with my own grief for which reason I haven't wanted to let it go. Because finishing up with that grief, I feel sometimes, is equivalent to letting go of the person place or thing that I've lost. And the grief is all I've got left. If the person is gone, at least I have them framed and preserved in my grief. Grief is interesting because it always gets our attention and if it doesn't, its inertia waxes until it can't be ignored anymore and demands expression. Sometimes that expression is illness.

And grief comes from places unexpected. We tend, in our minds, to relegate bereavement to the loss of a person or pet. But grief floats in our midst a vaporous cloud of uneasiness, *Weltschmerz* and angst that we never even notice until the pathologies, attendant with unexpressed grief, express themselves in our bodies and personalities: as diabolical as cancer; as seemingly innocuous as a facial tick. It's pretty easy to notice the various ways in which the pharmaceutical companies have answered to the call of grief-unexpressed. The unexpressed grief shows up as depression, sleeplessness, anxiety, anger, nervousness, lack of energy and probably even restless leg syndrome. It's the mother lode of social ills and the pharmaceutical companies, certainly on some level, know it. They build on it. And you know as well as I do, as Americans, we medicate before we ask the questions. Asking the questions means we've got to actually look at what's going on. We have to look at who we are: What we're becoming and where we're going. For many of us, in our busier than busy lives, we don't have the 'time' for it. To that end, the grief gets relegated to the temporary management zone using any one of the many anti-depressant drugs buffering us from grief's disabling presence in the body.

And, what about these American baby-boomers, of which I am a part? Were we not told that this country, the United States, was the greatest country in the world? That everyone wanted to live here? That this country was forged with the blood and sweat of our forefathers assuring us separation of church and state. That our unalienable rights: life, liberty and the pursuit of happiness would not and could not be taken from us. They were unalienable. Something happened while we were *busy* making money. Something happened while we were busy paying mortgages, surviving, burying our attention in our portfolios and arm-chair-warrioring through an endless number of brain-numbing cable channels. We were all busy, busy, busy.

The ideals faded. The urgent corporate and banking imperatives seemed to promote an agenda that eclipsed our basic rights. This courageous country's citizenry, for the most part, lost its courage and became complacent lulled by our computer screens while big business seized a golden egg which was our socio-political apathy circumscribed by overwhelm and exhaustion. The US government became the biggest of the big businesses. And this, in the wake of a president as recent as Harry Truman making 75,000 dollars a year. And what happened to us? We have been grieving the loss of those ideals ever since. We've been grieving the loss of real statesmanship in politics. We've been grieving the loss of our ability to manage our own health care in a way that is affordable. In short, many of us are grieving the loss of respectability in nearly every corner of our lives. Particularly as we age. This is a grief that has oozed into our lives with a kind of inexorability that has left us agitated and unnerved. With the exception of the Occupy movements, the sadness has continued unexpressed as the mood drugs pour off the assembly line and into our medicine cabinets.

And, how do we honor that sadness if this grief has no prescribed road map? How do we deal with losses so unprecedented. So treasonous. So incomprehensible. And so very heart-breaking?

Banks, financial institutions, our governing bodies, elected officials, healthcare, fiat currency, insurance companies. It's all smoke and mirrors. We know it, but tend to not want to accept it because it involves looking somewhere that invites endless questions. It involves revamping a world view. And revamping a world view, effectively, means starting at square one. And those questions can only anger, sadden and numb us. We watch stunned, bereft and broken as all of the structures upon which we'd hung our futures were blowing away like sand in the wind: IRAs, pensions and retirement programs. Scratching our heads about who to trust and what's real. Where do we put that grief and how on earth do we find the time to deal with these losses when we can barely pay all of our bills at the end of the month to a system we increasingly no longer have faith in. And like the twin towers disappearing into a surreal white cloud of powder on that fateful day with the images of "the jumpers" in our minds, our structures are coming down and we're scrambling to make sense of what is happening...as if we don't have enough going on. All of us lost a lot on that day. It bill-boarded for us the inevitability of changing times ahead. Now, many of us are "the jumpers". Jumping because the heat of stress is getting too intolerable.

And what about the loss of youth, vitality, ideals, love?? We've lost untold amounts over the years. But our culture doesn't create the time or space to honor those losses. And those stuck emotions manifest somehow. They manifest somewhere. It's an energetic axiom.

I don't believe I'm exaggerating when I say these things are staring at us in the face every day from the moment we get up in the morning. And every day we get busy so we don't have to square off with the enormity and intangibility of the sum of all our losses. I can tell you that it has been true for me.

In short, many of us have a sadness running just underneath our conscious thoughts. I know that it saddens me to think about all I've lost. And there's just so far anti-depressants, mood enhancers, pain relievers, sinus analgesics, allergy medicines, drugs and alcohol can take us before our bodies are reduced to a smoldering cinder of toxic waste. In my opinion, the taking of anti-depressants only forestalls the inevitable face off with the cause of the depression in the first place. And in most cases, we're worse off than when we started taking them. The way I see it, emotions are energy. And energy, like electricity, needs to move. When it doesn't move, it constipates the system in ways that are far more deleterious than the original emotion that was meant to be suppressed by drugs in the first place. So, the shortest distance between two points?:

> Dive headlong into the grief instead of putting it off, with pharmaceuticals, until it's really unmanageable. And what's so terribly wrong with sadness anyway? There is a sweetness contained in sadness. Songwriters, poets, painters and artists all know that the muse, more often than not, threads itself in the tapestry that is our sadness. And its grip releases its hold on us when we step into the middle of it rather than run from it.

The loss of my wife was horrible, horrible, horrible. It was 17 years ago and I lived through it. I was terribly sad. And that sadness is with me still, but it's something I can draw from. It's something that enriches my life. There is now a sweetness wrapped inside the sadness.

If there's one thing that's absolutely sure in this life, it's that we're going to lose some*one*, some*thing* and even, ultimately, our very breath. Yet we spend so much time and energy trying to deny that inevitability.

Yet loss is everywhere in nature. Does the tree mourn the loss of its leaves? Does the cliff mourn the loss of its rock as the ocean waves pound ceaselessly against it? Does the flower mourn the loss of it's beloved sun as it sinks below the horizon at the end of the day. Loss is part of life's very signature. So, why does it affect us so much?

Interestingly, at the same time I undertook to write this book about my own journey back to innocence, a writing partner and I decided we'd put the finishing touches on our book about grief and why it affected us so deeply.

We'd written the book 10 years ago about our common spousal losses. We wrote chapters of our own experiences through grief hoping that the two perspectives would offer up an interesting male and female view of loss. Jennifer had lost her husband less than a month after I'd lost my wife. We came to know each other while I was casting for a musical I'd written. Her son, Galen, was perfect for the part. Here is an excerpt I'd written from that book:

> *I walked down the aisle of the Methodist Church where Galen was with his mother. They were huddled around an ebony grand piano. I introduced myself to Galen and Jennifer. Galen looked like an English schoolboy. Porcelain and rosy-cheeked, he had the abstracted look. He avoided eye contact and hovered closely to his mom, seemingly frail and tentative*

> *"…Michael, and you are…Jennifer?"*

> *Her elegant frame stood beaten and unsure as we shook hands and took each other in. Her forehead was a topographical map that said, "How could this have happened to us?!" She seemed to be looking for energy from the piano…from the air she was breathing…anywhere she could get it.*

> *"And his Dad was your husband?"*

"Yes."

"When?" I asked.

"Beginning of December," she replied, *staring over my shoulder as if Gordon might suddenly appear there.*

"I lost my wife the 2nd of November."

We stared at one another as the tears welled. Reading each other, we recognized the familiar ache.

"You know, I'd...I'd just like to hear Galen sing a couple of intervals from the piano..." I said, breaking what would most surely have become a chain reaction of tears.

"...We have a song he could sing for you," she interjected.

"Well, that would be great...you can accompany him?"

She nodded.

Jennifer sat at the piano like it was an old friend. And this friend seemed to hold her together. She sat with an elegance and command of the instrument. And the piano knew, like a horse knows about its rider, that she was now in control. The piano was an extension of the unarticulated part of herself. The part that had no words, and if it did, would need be in Sanskrit or Aramaic.

Jennifer gave Galen a nod that it was "ok" to sing now. Galen's voice had the bell-like ring of a Viennese choirboy. He sang with impeccable pitch and a stunningly accurate British accent. It was a song from The Secret Garden. He became that innocent English boy to escape the impossibly difficult task of being a Southern Oregon boy who'd just lost his father. His ethereal strains flew high above his own earthbound grief. Watching the boy beneath him on an island of loss and despair, the ruddy-cheeked boy overhead circled as he soared and dipped through the clouds. The tones, like the pure sound coming from a fine crystal goblet struck by a felt hammer, hung in every rosewood corner of the church. Winging his way in the company of cherubs and angels, a fanfare of trumpets announced the coming of this joyous choirboy. With a final dive, the winged boy became one with the Galen standing close to his mother at the piano. Galen looked up, though not at me, when he finished singing. The flight was over. He was back in the body. He was back in the impossible thick of it.

"I think he'd do great...is he available for rehearsal early next..."

As I was speaking, I was seeing this woman collapsing before my eyes. Galen stood by her as if to prop her up. They were both being strong for each other, Galen more on autopilot than his mom. They seemed like a J.D. Salinger mother and son team, bound together by blood, common experience, and an uncommon sensitivity borne of keen intelligence.

---from Maya and the Gordian Knot (J.
Schloming - M. Mish)

Here I am embarking on uncovering all the things that stripped me of my innocence by turning my life upside down, and revisiting this book, and all the experiences it referenced, could not have been more perfectly serendipitous. I re-read the pages of the 10 year old manuscript and the reading still found me with tears on my face. Reading, again, about my wife and how I'd missed her, was just as alive for me as it was at the time of its writing.

Am I still grieving the loss of my wife? Am I still grieving the loss of the dreams associated with that loss? We were planning on having a child. We were planning on moving to Port Townsend on Washington's Olympic Peninsula. We were in the planning stages of a marriage barely 3 months old when she was torn from my life. In spite of all the conscious grief work I've done about the loss, it is still as fresh as if it had happened last night. I have not finished! I haven't finished grieving and probably never will!

The important aspect here is that I am looking at and examining this grief. I see it when it rears its head. I see it when it tries to dictate choices about future relationships (is she going to die too...this woman I'm now interested in?). And noticing is important. Clearly, when I notice the past moving into my present moment, I have the choice to allow it to dictate its warning or I can choose to simply see it as an experience and an influence.

As I am in Switzerland and Jennifer is in Southern Oregon, the mere mention of additional revisions cause our Skype-faces and Skype-voices to droop with world-weariness. There's no getting around it, grief is always tugging at me, but how I allow it to impinge on my peace...that is a choice.

I've seen the marks of grief etched in people's foreheads. Why, hell, I even see it in my own face. It greets me each morning.

"Hello, I am the crease in your forehead, how are you today?"

"Yeah, yeah..." I say.

"Ah, not so well, I see. You have a crease in your forehead."

And the grief rabbit hole goes as deep as I'm willing to follow it. There are all the losses and all the attendant unobserved griefs associated with them: Not the least of which, I think most of us grieve the loss of our own innocence. And that loss, like any loss, lives together with a life long string of separations, deaths and estrangements.

When my brother's pet rat was liberated from its cage by our 5-year old next door neighbor only to liberate my pet turtle of its head, I was thrust into a vertiginous and spinning world of rage and grief at the injustice of it all. I cried for hours as my world crumbled beneath me. You'd think my heart had been ripped from my chest. The image of my turtle's headless remains seared in my brain for months following. The world of a child, and I was around 7 at the time, is immersed in a richness that is not always readily noticed or appreciated by adults. My parents looked at me, bewildered and were probably thinking, "What's the big deal, here?" But the turtle for me was a best friend. A friend I confided in. A friend that never questioned, ridiculed or criticized. That turtle filled out my world.

That's the way loss works. If you grieve one loss, you're grieving them all. And there are many.

Many losses.

The Gift in Loss

What eludes many of us, though, is the invitation that loss offers. For me, the losses were bookmarks posing the inevitable question: who am I without this person; this animal or this thing? It stops us cold in our tracks and demands an examination of all that we've lost up to that point. When I lost my girlfriend, when I was 19, I had to look at all that I'd lost since the loss of my turtle – at age 7 -- not because I wanted to, but because I *had* to. And, when I lost my wife, I grieved all of it – all over again with the addition of another 2 decades of little losses. With these re-examinations of a life, comes an up-dated assessment of who we are now. Instead of pulling along a long train of worn out identities from the past, those identities are set free. Now we can ask:

Who am I without my wife?

Who am I without my job?

Who am I without my hair?

Who am I now?

And this is an important question. The unavoidable conclusion is that there is something underneath the vestment that is the role of Father or Mother or Scientist or Clergyman. We are not our roles. We are not our job. We are not our house, our beliefs, our identities or the losses themselves. We are something far grander than any of these impossibly narrow ideas of ourselves would seem to suggest.

Stress

Stress, on the other hand, is the ultimate thief. Robbing us of our time and our peace.

In a 1983 edition of Time Magazine, the cover story dubbed stress *The Epidemic of the 80's*. Think how your life has changed in the last *10* years. Has it gotten more stressful? And who is even questioning where this phantom stress comes from? We seem to be in solemn acceptance of it as if it's part of the deal. We unquestioningly accept that it's part of life and making a living. And, in an act of societal perversion, we've even made it a cultural value. As if to be in a constant state of barely manageable stress is a badge of courage of sorts. Stress has become the drum-beat of our generations. We even compete with one another to see whose life is most stressful. It's as if our society even rewards stress. Yet, an astounding 75 to 90% of all visits to primary care physicians are stress related illnesses. Where it was called the epidemic of the 80's, today stress is considered "The Silent Killer".

"Where does the time go?"

"There aren't enough hours in a day."

"I'm overwhelmed."

And for those of us who have the foresight to see stress in our lives as the heart attack waiting to happen that it actually is, we try meditation, sports, mood drugs, (all too permissively prescribed by doctors in my opinion) food, alcohol, recreational drugs and you name it. But who even thinks of eliminating the *cause* of the stress to begin with? We just figure it's the price of having a wonderful life (which is an interesting irony all by itself). Having a stressful job or a stressful role in the family is the *cost* of having a wonderful life in the most privileged country on earth. We are so well off. We are so lucky. We are so affluent.

Then, without warning, one of our friends dies. We wonder what it's all about. How a life could come and go. Does this person still exist in some form. What is life anyway: energy and consciousness? Is our friend still conscious? What happened to this person's consciousness after their body had been reduced to a white-gray powder with bits of bone fragment nestled in a plastic bag with a zip tie. And. That's enough.

No more.

I'm not going to think about this. It's too sad. It's too dark.

Enough time spent at wondering what it's all about. It's no longer pleasant to think about or muse over. Death is just too damned scary. Get rid of it. Bury it under the ground. Cast it out to sea. Give it to the Minister to explain away. Let the crematorium handle it. Someone deal with it.

I can't deal with this right now. It's too stressful.

Go to a country, though, that is poor and has seemingly none of the privileges we have in the West and they seem a lot happier than we do. They have easy-going and relaxed natures. And we ask ourselves, "Why am I living this fast-paced life when I could be living here? Oh yeah, I almost forgot...the stuff! All the great stuff I have!"

Stress is said to sponsor:

Asthma, obesity, hypertension, headaches, irritable bowel syndrome, high blood-pressure, rheumatoid arthritis, insomnia, chronic fatigue, ulcers, cancer and, likely, several others. But even more importantly stress undermines the body's immune response over time, and the body's immune system is our first line of defense against illness.

In my own life, stress is at the seat of all my disturbances. And I've seen the behavioral patterns repeating themselves over and over that try compensating for the stress:

Staying busy

Keeping entertained

Throwing myself into a project to keep me distracted

Where is innocence when all this stuff is going on? It's hiding beneath the stuff. That's where it is.

What I Did about the Stress

I took a hard look at the things keeping me from being happier and more easy-going and I chose to begin with looking at, and eliminating, the stress in my life.

Quite simply, every expectation on me was stressful. (My *own* expectations preeminently.)

Nearly every responsibility I had that didn't seem like something I deeply wanted to do was stressful:

Mortgages

Medical insurance

Credit card

These little bundles of stress were installed everywhere in my life. Taken alone, they were manageable. When grouped together, they amalgamated into a menacing and furry monster that enslaved me. I was surrounded by these stress monsters. And, why did I allow this accumulation of stress to be there in the first place?: This was what I needed to deal with in order to have a comfortable life. But stress was keeping me from actually *being* comfortable. But, this is what you do. This is what you do because everyone else is doing it. This is what is deemed acceptable...the norm...inescapable...the whole gnarly deal.

This is what you do.

Sure. I knew I could choose to look at these things differently and with a peacefully beatific smile on my face, re-frame the stress. I could calmly perfume my perspective of the stress. I could do yoga, meditate and exercise more. I could 'manage' it better.

OR.

I could take the General Patton approach and obliterate even the remotest suggestion of stress in my life.

Looking out my bedroom window, I watched as the same alder trees swayed back and forth lolling gently in the wind. Sixteen years prior, my wife had died. I'd been looking at those trees through that bedroom window for very nearly as long. Was another sixteen years going to pass by as I chased my tail trying to make money. Would I be lying here in another ten years looking at the same trees wondering the same thing? Certainly the last sixteen years blitzed by. And they say: "The older we get, the faster time flies." How could it go by any faster? Faster than the wink of an eye. Then it's over. And with my last gasp, I'd wonder, "What happened? Where did the time go?" Not enough hours in a day. Not enough days in a life. And I was just doing what I did. Doing what one does. I was doing all the right things!

Deconstructing the Stress

a Radical Socio-Ectomy

There was one thing I could do right away. I could even start the same day. Convinced that I wouldn't sit still while the remaining years of my life were whisked away under time's cloak of darkness, I decided on a radical socio-ectomy of sorts and I would begin with stress and its eradication. The elimination of stress had to be looked at, as though, through a surgeon's eyes. Donning the most objective and Teutonic lens on my surroundings, I looked at everything in my life. I looked at my habits. I looked at my possessions. My beliefs. I looked at my house.

Hmmm. Did I dare?

Ridding myself of habits stood to be a nebulous and somewhat long-term and bedraggled affair that dealt with a deliberate re-wire of the brain and reckoning with those pesky and rigid neural pathways. Breaking bad habits take time. They take introspection and a near military determinism. But, the house and all the things contained within it?

Yes.

That was something tangible. That was something I could DO. So, I set out to rid myself of nearly all possessions. As an environmental spokesperson, I'd spoken to children for years about reducing, reusing and recycling. Now, finally, I was going to radically practice what I preached for all those years. I wanted to *reduce* my possessions to nothing.

The things in my house contrived to spell out who I was. And from the oddest of odd arithmetical view points: "I" was the sum total of all I possessed. The mechanics of this notion, from a well-greased social collective and consumerist point of view, is masterfully conceived. It makes for an active and healthy nation of commerce and jobs. On some level, though, it just wasn't serving me as a person. The 'not enough' belief set, seemed to me, a disease and an addiction. Nothing was enough. It could never be enough because few, if any of us, ever really got what we wanted. We're a nation condemned to act out Citizen Cane's obsession with his "Rosebud". We didn't get what we needed in the first few years of our lives, so we look for that childhood dream inside a clanking assortment of cars We look for it in the next latest and greatest time-saving device driven by an urge to satisfy our obsession with technophilia. We look for it in clothes or whatever else.

Frankly, and as a side-note, I feel American consumerism essentially lives on the back of the have-nots: the working masses in under-developed countries. Though I'd thought through this Western aberration hundreds of times, I'd never actually set the wheels in motion to do anything about it.

Was I going to submit to being a ticking immune-system-time-bomb waiting for an anatomical system failure? Cancer? Heart-disease? Drug-resistant staff infection? Blood clot? And what, really, had kept me here in this stressful situation? Trying to make a living? Trying to pay money into a home mortgage's gaping maw? The predictability of it all was enough to prompt a decision then and there to sell everything. And sell it all, I did.

The Mother of All Stressors

And what about the perceived not-enoughs? After all, I only had all this "stuff" because I, in all likelihood, felt I didn't have enough of something:

Not enough money, friends, love, sex, power, status, possessions or respect.

I probably felt I wasn't smart; good-looking; intelligent; lovable or fit enough.

And the stealthiest of all killer beliefs:

I didn't feel enough.

The not-enough circus for me was the mother of all stressors and it was sponsored by the original sin:

Not feeling, as Jean Liedloff would enthusiastically concur, worthy or welcome.

~

To strip away all the comforts and familiarities of home, possessions and, to a degree, my support group of friends, was a radical and nearly brutal step. But it was going to have to be a fairly extreme repositioning to get me to snap out of it. I needed to wake up from the ease and complacency of the middle class, middle aged and middle minded death trap. I'd chosen to be seduced by the creature comforts, but the comforts themselves had a sinister and rapacious consequence. And, I had to pay no small price. I needed to be simple again like I came in because with nothing else to distract and confuse me, there was only one choice. And that choice was to walk through the fire. Naked again.

Hamelin Bay, W. Australia - 2012

CHAPTER 18

The Naked Passage

EVERY SHAMAN, WORTH his salt, knows that there is one way and one way only to finesse being on the outside of the cultural box looking in, and that involves being totally naked. We come in naked. We go out naked. And the passage into a new way of living, loving and believing also asks us to be stripped down, vulnerable, and defenseless. Like a baby.

This was one grand gesture I could make. Maybe if I got rid of everything I owned, my mind would get the message that I would still be OK – but, with less stuff. If I could get the mind feeling good about that, then I'd convince my mind that it would *also* be alright to get rid of the emotional stuff consisting of the beliefs and the identities. But, baby steps. I didn't want to overwhelm the mind with too much new information. My mind, in the past anyway, has been a well-defended place -- The province and protected territory of my ego. Throwing too much at it at one time has a dizzying effect on the ego and, in the true style of a lawyer, the ego's default position is "no".

The idea of a "stuff divestiture" had a surprising element of sentimentality. Every object, like every person, has its story. And every object's story, curiously, identified me in a time and space. By that I mean, I had a vague memory of where and when I got the toaster, the spatula, the tool box, and the door-stop. And all of them would call out my name as I'd pass by them in the kitchen, bedroom and garage. For, even though I may have fancied myself as non-materialistic, I found that I was heavily identified with each object I owned. Not only with the object itself, but with its *condition* and its functionality...not that I consciously wanted to be. When my computer had a virus, I felt like I was sick. When the car didn't run, my life was out-of-sync and immobilized. When a kitchen chair had a broken leg, it made my home imperfect and I couldn't relax until it was fixed.

The notion of casting off everything I owned was too radical. Too anti-social. Too counter-culture. Too much at variance with the-sum-total-of-all-I-was-ever-taught.

Too perfect.

So I began.

I started small: The clothes I hadn't worn in a year. The technical things like stray AC chargers. Redundant extension cords. Crock pots. Bread-maker. Old juicer. Out-dated vitamins. The more I got rid of, the more I wanted to get rid of. Worked up into a get-rid-of-it-all-lather, I cleaned out cupboards and garage shelves of never-used items with brutal sweeps of the hand into a plastic bag. The activity alone felt like a psychic purge as I continued feeling lighter.

The system to the full-fledged divestiture? I would liberate my things on 4 different launch pads of relocation:

- The Garage Sale

- Give-away

- Throw-away (the old, decrepit, and decomposing)

- Sell off

The Garage Sale

As American as apple pie, and a great way to meet interesting people as well as scavengers of every description, the garage sale was a major step. In my case, it was made into something fun with the help of neighbors bending over backwards to help out. I never ever knew just how neighborly my neighbors could be. The, otherwise, courteous nameless faces going about their businesses now, rallied to help, to advise, however they could. I wondered why *now*. Now, that I was selling everything. Only now was I meeting this friendly, out-going group of people. I figured this kind of camaraderie only shows up when there's a unifying local tragedy, or a fire, or an act of terrorism...or, a garage sale. Neighbors can be fantastic. With their help, the drudgery became a delightful game. In my case, it was like the lyric:

**In every job that must be done,
there is an element of fun.[1]**

The following days found me Mary Poppin-ning around my house sticking price tags on everything for the "opening day" of my garage sale. It was like mounting a musical before the curtain going up on opening night. There was:

The 5 cent basket.

The electronics corner.

The kitchen corner.

The record albums and CD corner.

The music and video studio corner of endless adapters and cables

The automotive supply nook

Little price tags were stuck on nearly everything. The garage sale signs announcing this one-time event not-to-be-missed were, alternately, tied or stapled on all 4 corners (every conceivable approach to my subdivision). Yes. This was as close to the circus as I would ever see in Ashland, Oregon. People of all cultures, shapes and sizes trying on their business acumen with a near startling, and sometimes off-putting, aplomb.

The garage sale convention was not to be taken seriously. No. People would haggle for pennies off the give-away price. Whatever penchant we have for haggling, completely lost in our western culture, comes out with a vengeance

[1] *A Spoonful of Sugar* by Richard and Robert Sherman (Mary Poppins)

in the garage sale. Nothing is sacred. And the 'good' deal is the only motivator. I'm now convinced. People will buy anything, if it's a good deal.

All the "things" that didn't get relocated from the garage sale found other homes through the wonder of stuff-purgatories; the patron saint of all people turning their lives upside down: The Goodwill. The Goodwill was happy to accept this endless train of boxes and bags that no one else wanted. There seemed to be a "stuff" food chain. At the bottom of said chain, there was The Goodwill. And, like the Salvation Army in earlier years, I was thankful to them. They seem to stand silently by as I move through these various incarnations. There is something saintly about them and I'll forever be grateful.

Give Away

"Hey, Richard. 'You have any use for this pair of speakers?"

"Well, yeah, but are you sure…"

"…Yes. I'm sure."

Many of my possessions went to friends that gave me the 'worried look' of:

"Do you really mean to be doing this?"

"Are you sure you want to give this to me. Aren't you going to need this again at some point?"

At some point, maybe, but I'm not going to horde all this shit for "some point's" eventuality. Nope. It was all going. Every thread. Every needle. Every *thing*.

End of story. It seems that most people are happy to have your stuff. And I was happy to give it to them.

Throw-away

I found much of the stuff I had was recyclable so I let the blessed recycling pickup guys fling my bounty of booty in their truck on every Monday's pickup.

Sell off

The alder trees swayed in a unified Greek chorus encouraging me onward as I systematically put the house up for sale. Most every 'thing' in the house I prepared for its listing on E-Bay or Craigslist. Nearly overnight, once the house sold, my house became an assembly line. Taking pictures of everything I was selling, I wrote copy for every precious object that I was liberating from my home with a Madison Avenue slick. Interestingly, I often described how very attached I was to the object, describing its months or years of dutiful service. With everything for sale, the living room became a vertical packing and shipping operation. I was both foreman and worker. Janitor and shipping clerk.

As all the personal effects marched out of the house, I watched the emotions swell and recede: an undulating Loch Ness creature stitching the emotional lake's placid cold water. The feelings rose out of a past that I was curiously growing unattached to. It was someone else's life calling out to me and I resisted its call – not without affection but with a stolid resolve to sever all ties. The most compelling tugs were associated with the little things that were given to me as gifts. The ceramic angel figurine my wife had since birth. (I know, I know, I should've given it to her mother...but her mother wanted me dead and there was no time to go there. No time.) The birthday cards. The jumper cables. All these objects with which I would no longer be identified. I elatedly declared that I was not the birthday cards. I was not my jumper cables. Hell, the objects themselves didn't care one way or the other, but I'd, somehow, managed to superimpose feelings on all of them – personifying them into things they were never meant, or able, to be:

When I wasn't even looking, I'd become my shirts, my electric keyboard, my essential oils. I'd become my books, and my thumbtacks. I was a patchwork quilt of disparate objects strewn all around my house. These were artifacts in a mausoleum celebrating the life of someone I wasn't even sure I knew anymore.

I kept reminding myself that I could always replace this thing with another 'new-fangled' iteration of itself if I needed to. But the difference would be that my future purchases would, hopefully, reflect a more seasoned discretion: A more updated representation of the person I had become. I would buy this thing because I actually needed it. I would buy it because it had real utility in a real way. This is very different from having imported this or that item into the present moment because it was important to me at *some* point in the past. And for me, I had dozens of things from my 20's. And it was time to place these things into the stuff-conga-line and watch as they step-step-step-kicked out of my front door.

Tears welled. There were, in fact, a bountiful supply of tears. But for me, tears are both right and good. There is joy intermingled with the sadness in closing a chapter. Like all stories -- all human stories. In all time and space. They are our stories. Personally, I love these stories. They make rich the pallet of human emotion. They are the stories of human kind. They are the universal stories etched into the genome. The sadness and the joy get reflected in our art, our music and our history.

And as the divestiture continued, I felt like more. Not less.

My objective was the moon. The moon was urging me homeward. So, I was simply clearing the decks to allow the moon to shine more brightly. More purely. So I could see and experience the wonder of wonders. The wonder of the "Ooom". Again.

Colonia, Uruguay - 2008

CHAPTER 19

Where To?

M Y FIRST THOUGHTS were to simply go back to Uruguay, a country I'd visited before and liked, and begin again. New language. New faces. New sites. New hemisphere of the planet. New hemisphere of the brain. The prospects were, at once, tinged with excitement, and dread (hell...I could be unimaginably lonely). Pushing the two lobes of the brain to cross-connect using languages, music, different careers and what not...is ONE thing. But starting over at 60 is quite another! 60 is when most of us are lulled into the comfortable thing. The soft couch. The soft bed. The soft routine. The soft belly. Coasting on the financial successes of the past. Not so. Not so, anymore. It had become a different world for me and most of my friends. The retirement nest eggs were fast becoming dreams of a world, far, far away. The notion that we stay mentally active longer had become more a necessity than something we did for amusement. And this is probably going to emerge as being the de facto way of the future rather than the option. More of us will need to come out of retirement or simply not take our retirement. I feel the enviro-disasters in the Gulf of Mexico, Fukushima and the game-changing erosion of global financial institutions coupled with the power shift from West to East, are going to necessitate an examination of our lives and futures in a very different way.

Certainly, what came up for me was:

I'm getting older, so why would I want to put myself in more uncertainty? What could I do to make a living if I'm starting over this "late" in the game? With whom would I be spending the final years of my life? Where will financial security come from?!

For me, there was no option. The inevitable was looking more and more like:

Growing old was going to consist of standing helplessly by as a failing financial system systematically stripped me of every last shred of a retirement possibility and respectability.

This scenario was not an option.

Responsive *to* and programmed *by* my social group, the largest single challenge facing me was the prospect of floating off into societal oblivion – all because I knew I was making a conscious choice to sever all connections between me and that which is socially known, acceptable and safe. In doing so, I have exposed myself to all sorts of uncertainties.

There was something so completely red pill/blue pill-ish about a decision like this. The risk was gigantic. We all know, though, that there is a direct relationship between the degree of risk and the degree of payoff.

~

> The holy grail of innocence emerges as both the result and reward to unplugging. And, in my opinion, innocence is the greatest thing we can aspire to.

~

All great things happen on the seams of our awareness. I could not be more fully convinced of this. We are all aware of the innumerable examples of discoveries, inventions and eureka ideas that have occurred...not during the waking state, rather in some version of a half-waking state or dream. And I was about to thrust myself back onto the seams of reality. I was about to travel and live in that fringe-like world that most people only do when they take a vacation. For me it had become a way of life -- A way to keep society's glue from sticking to me. I was about to live on the seams again -- That rich, un-ballasted, terrifying, limitless, orgasmic, delightful and diabolical veil.

Of Dreams and Seams

The most recorded song in music history, "Yesterday", came to Paul McCartney in a dream.

Elias Howe's sewing machine was perfected in a dream.

Thomas Edison knew exactly where his inventions were given birth: the half-waking state. He was said to have routinely taken naps in his chair with a ball bearing clutched in his hand suspended over a tin pie plate. When he'd fall asleep, the ball bearing would fall from his limp hand, hitting the pie plate, and the clatter would wake him up and he'd promptly write down what was on his mind in that moment.

The hypnagogic, or threshold consciousness state, is the terrain that is well known by artists and dreamers. It even has a kind of sacredness wrapped around it for them. Even most of *us* have said, when we need to make an important decision, "Let me sleep on it". It's this world between worlds, the veil, that beckons us home to reclaim what is rightfully and, somehow, divinely our providence. And this is what I long for when I see a child living in that rich and colorful world: Because their imaginative universe hasn't yet embraced a consensus reality.

As with the shaman making the precipitous journey back to his essential self, there is always an element the suggests a brush with death. And that death, from my perspective, can be death of the ego or a physical death. In either case it represents a dis-identification with the body as being the source of the self. In my own experience, my having had a nervous breakdown at 19 and the loss of my wife at 44 were tantamount to 'deaths'. These experiences put me in a state where I was not concerned if I died or not. In both cases, I stood before a black maelstrom as it swirled with its laconic entreaty: "It's ok, step in". And I knew that stepping into it was *some* kind of death. At those moments, I was utterly fearless standing in the face death. And, while the thought is 3 degrees left of macabre, its mere possibility was perfectly and exquisitely freeing. I'd go so far as to say that freedom isn't even possible if there is a fear of death. And being a part of this Western culture, I know just how obsessive we are in our fear of death and dying. We covet all things youthful to help us believe that:

This body's not going to die. Others will; this body won't. I'm going to cheat death.

Overcoming that fear of death causes the veil to lift: Yet, we die to our 'reality' when we go to sleep and we die to our dreams when we awaken. This is the veil that the shaman knows all too well. The veil that the person dying in a hospital bed knows. The veil that a person experiencing a near-death experience knows because the experience has changed his life forever. But what a deliciously heady notion to live on a stage without worrying about death's inevitability all the time! Death is not the end, it's the end of a chapter and the beginning of a new one. Isn't it?!

Then there's living *on* the veil itself – the razor's edge skirting life and death. The 'edge' that mountain climbers, inching their way up a sheer rock face, know about. The edge that extreme skiers know by heart. The edge that surfers know staring at eternity in the blue tube. And as addictive and tempting as this razor's edge is, it is not the enduring edge enjoyed by the meditator, inventor or artist that conditions his brain and his impulses to withdraw mentally from his conditioned responses in the waking state.

Living *on* the veil, instead of living on one side of it, seems to resound with the impossible and deafening quiet of a moment's eternality. This is where, I'm guessing, innocence lives. Can a baby 'think' about death? Decidedly not. Without the fear of death, an entire world of wonder shows up. And it did for me both times. The fear of death virtually disappeared during the nervous breakdown (as uncomfortable and vertiginous as it was) and after the loss of my wife. I was swept up in a strange fearlessness, but one that I was ill-prepared for. I was neither strong nor brave enough to deal with all that living on the veil entailed. I wasn't trained in the ways of fearlessness. As the shaman would probably say, it is a long and disciplined path to be able to negotiate the demands of living a life with a foot in each world. Because to have a foot in each world, unplugging from the societal matrix, is not a choice it's a necessity.

Why would I figure innocence to be the result of unplugging? Why not simply 'freedom' or 'sovereignty' or a kind of Emersonian 'self-reliance'?

Because different from either freedom, sovereignty or self-reliance, innocence has embedded within it the universally sought euphoria of experiencing things for the first time. And in the strictest sense, can any of us ever, ever, ever see something the same way twice. No. It's the brain that makes the assumption that:

"I've already seen a toothbrush."

"I've already driven down this road."

"I've already been to Alaska."

"I've already been married."

"I've already run a marathon."

"I've already told her I love her."

For if the one thing we CAN count on is change, then indeed we've never seen this toothbrush the same way twice. It's already had hundreds of millions of photons pass through it. It's reflecting the bathroom light in a way different than before. The bristles are more splayed than they were a few days ago. We're ALWAYS seeing the world around us anew. We just don't know it. But to consciously experience the world around us as something wondrously new, we'd be lost in a confounding overwhelm of constantly processing information. The brain, therefore like a computer, paves a short cut for us.

The left brain is constantly 'file-saving' and grouping like-information into zip-files so the amount of information can be kept simplified and ordered. With every "been there/done that" assumption that the brain makes, we're being denied the discovery in that moment. I know that if I dive into the center of the moment, I can potentially find eternity there. I, similarly, find innocence. I find that innocence in the sweetness of meditation. I find innocence in the rose. It's actually everywhere I care to look and notice it.

To take the time to meditate or to take in the incomparable sweetness of the rose, is to take time *outside* of the busy, reality-adjusted world of man.

Crater Lake, Oregon - 2007

CHAPTER 20

Waving Goodbye

THIS WAS MY last day in Oregon. I would springboard from the known into the unknown. It wasn't until 9pm or so that night of December 20th that I'd gotten the last thing out of the house. My house, once vibrating with life, was now a mere shell awaiting another inhabitant. The house twitched ghostly in the pale yellow tract housing light. Its mouth agape, it was trying to catch its breath after being punched in the stomach with the imminent departure of its faithful friend and inhabitant of 10 years. Joanna and Donnelly arrived as I handed over the keys to them. They'd asked if we could encourage ceremony out of what was basically a dry transaction. The house, and all its obligations, lifted from my shoulders with that singular and symbolic handing over of the keys. I hugged them both and very *un*ceremoniously opened my car door half hoping that they'd ask me to stay there with them. Unsure, sleep-deprived and travel-weary, I looked at them as I poked my head out of the car window as a few snow flakes collected on my eye lashes. This was my first experience at not having a house to live in since the Salvation Army experience of 40 years ago. Oh cruel December. Everything strange happened in November and December. Thieves of daylight. Harbingers of the darkness. November – the traitorous assassin of our marriage. Those very dark months leaving nothing much to ever look forward to. December was sitting on me, a dispassionate and cold weight on my chest. As I looked into the soft eyes of these magnificent people, I so regretted never having gotten to know them before they bought my house.

Driving off, they waved to me. Looking back over my left shoulder as I slowly made my way down the street I'd jogged on thousands of times, I could see them, arm in arm, waving goodbye. Partially illuminated on the porch by the light from the living room, this sweet couple were my parents as I was being born to a new life. That thought made me burst into tears. My tires squeaked against the thin layer of freshly fallen snow. The street lights loomed like enormous and translucent pulsing yellow disks as my wet eyes saw this dear couple in my side view mirror get swallowed up by the night and the falling snowflakes.

I drove into the night convulsing at the wheel thinking of all the people I was leaving. Those I loved. Donna. My amazing neighbors helping me. Supporting me. My best friends of 40 years in some cases. My family. And a whole community that watched as I stumbled and fell and then got up again. I thought of my father who had passed away just 2 years before. I could finally take him on a trip with me because, on this adventure, he'd be in my heart.

I arrived at a friend's house near the airport. Eerily, strangely, and completely spent from the endless last minute bagging of trash and cleaning the house, I fell into bed unraveled, and tumbled into a fitful sleep.

Early the next morning, I boarded a plane for Western Australia.

And, that's when the real traveling began. The journey of having no identity, possessions or direction.

Near Walpole, W. Australia - 2012

CHAPTER 21

Waltzing into the Void

MY FRIEND, BRAD, was stricken with a near fatal disease. I'd heard about it from someone else also living in Ashland. A prior neighbor, Brad had worked on remodeling my parents' house nearly 18 years before and, since then, I'd seen him in town only on rare occasions. At the time of the news, I hadn't been in contact with Brad for some time. So it is with most things in Ashland, you think about the person and they appear. I was in the market getting last minute groceries. There he was in shorts. He always wore shorts. Even when I was bundled up in a down jacket, Brad wore shorts. Summer, Fall, Winter, Spring: Shorts.

"This thing's made me a believer," he said referring to his disease. "There were these women at the church where I was working, and they were praying for me. I heard they'd been praying for me and I thought 'that's awesome...awesome they'd pray for me,'" he continued. "And while those women were in a meeting in the chapel, I walked in there to say hello to them and these ladies that had kept me in their prayers looked at me. And I felt like I was being held. Like they were holding me up." Brad always had a smile on his face when he talked. But I'd never seen tears welling in his eyes before. Never when he'd speak about his wife or kids would he have tears in his eyes. Brad was over six feet tall, unflappable with a big "aw shucks" kid about him. But tears were filling in his eyes. "I felt like I was small and all these ladies were holding me, and it was like nothing I've ever felt before." He looked to his shoes, then slowly back to me. "I think they healed me," he said, his smile fading to serious. His mouth, a little unsteady.

I'd never seen him serious like that. Ever.

"I think they healed me and that's why I'm alive. They're why I'm here," he said.

There was silence because I was trying to calm the tightening knot in my throat and quell the tears about to flow. He stared at me looking for an answer.

"I've never known an experience like that before. They were sitting over there, but they were holding me in their arms."

That's what *I* felt when these women descended on my home to help me sell it, decorating and dressing it up as only a woman can. That's what I felt when these neighborhood women helped me clean my house. That's what I felt when they helped me organize the garage sales and helped me to give away countless possessions that I was just too overwhelmed to deal with. They knew I had to sell everything and move. They knew I stood on a precipice of a huge life change. They could feel it from me. They saw the need, and felt moved to help me.

They held me in an embrace softer and more sublime than any physical embrace I'd known.

They healed me. They healed a spirit that felt frayed, worthless, beaten and overwhelmed. I will be forever grateful to these intrepid take-charge women that moved in to birth a new chapter in my life. And they did it with the expertise of skilled midwives. Like Brad, I'm here because of them.

Not unlike the way in which I was held and supported by my neighbors when I was moving, I was similarly welcomed by several families and former friends while traveling. These friends were sacred to me. Born to this new reality of no possessions, I began boarding planes and visiting friends I'd met from previous trips.

There were the families that took me in while traveling. I similarly felt held by them. And as I embarked at once on the traveler's ever-changing surround and the world of all possibility, I felt valued and loved by these people. And the former relationship I'd had with them, whether it was from 4 months prior or from over 40 years ago, it was revivified once more. As I stepped off a train or emerged from customs, our eyes met and whatever time had elapsed melted away under the radiance of our, once again, familiar smiles.

"You haven't changed at all."

"Neither have you..."

"...I can't wait to catch up."

That frozen moment when the smile and twinkle in the eye dissolved time, was what I so looked forward to. We picked up where we'd left off. And there it was again. Those faces, open in a timeless recognition, were like welcome mats. Whatever trepidation I might have had about traveling, promptly evaporated in the shelter of their caring. In this journey of stripping myself down to get back to a more innocent essence, it was made clearer than ever that: nothing is more important than friends.

Nothing.

The friendships skipped over time and space reminding me that everything that is truly important in life is, likewise, eternal. The truly significant things elude the measuring stick of time and space because they defy being quantified. Somehow, though, I've managed to lose a number of, even close, friends since my 'socio-ectomy'. And that has been a very difficult one to deal with.

Though nearly every friend in my life has been the result of some kind of "chance" meeting, I couldn't help but think that chance had nothing to do with it. We constellate the skies of our lives with who we need when we need them. And those friends appear. It's a kind of airy fairy axiom that actually works.

But, it's the ones that endure time and the many changes in our lives that are the gems. And I am so grateful to them.

Drama

Invariably, however, as I would move more closely into their lives, the little dramas would emerge. Being on the outside and looking in as a visitor and as someone living life on the fringe, the personal and inter-family dramas were more obvious to me than ever.

And as I'd listen with a compassionate ear, I could feel myself not being drawn in. Not feeling personally responsible. Not feeling part of it. I also noticed that it didn't diminish my concern for the situations...as difficult, dramatic or gut wrenching as the stories may have been. This was something very different for me and I observed my friends' stories with a clinician's objectivity. Perhaps not having the knee-jerk penchant for entering into the dramas was the result of giving up all my stuff. Maybe there was something to it: You give away your physical stuff, and the psychic stuff begins to fall away as well – and without any coaxing.

Many of the people I met, though, were married to their stories. They even defined themselves by the stories they steadfastly clung to as being real. And the stories seemed to be based on the most available situations like: there never being enough parking; an errant son or daughter; the changing city-scape; the dog; the produce; the air. Not being a part of the cultural story enabled me to see these dramas strictly as an outsider such that, in retrospect, I was able to size up my own personal myths and imagined challenges. Stories add color to a life. And I love them. For me, it's important to know when the story is running the show or simply being a source of entertainment – two different things entirely.

I can only call it fascinating. Fascinating because I found that I'd always needed a story to cling to in the past. Fascinating because I wasn't able to be satisfied without having something to complain about. Observing others complaining about all and sundry shed light on why I'd clung so fixedly to my beliefs that suggested I had problems.

There were no real problems.

I had no real problems.

If I had a problem at all, it was with my own inner-critic.

Watching the unbelievably stern self-assessments crop up, I'd think I was being tried by a humorless, merciless and brittle judge. And, finally, I am the judge. What would possess me to be so very ruthless with myself? At times, I was more judgmental of myself than the most formidable enemy. Why did my friends seem to indulge the self-same auto-critic?

And, nearly, without exception, each friend had themselves on their own chopping block. And the sponsors of these criticisms?: their stories about who they were. I felt that shame and not-enough-ness were at the bottom of every self castigation...every story...every drama.

I felt that I needed to take a closer look at my own inner-critic and shame issues to be freed from this, the most hidden of all, joy killers: The inner critic and its whip of shame.

Doomed at Birth

Ideally, oxytocin (the love hormone) is released from the mother's brain at the time of birth. Mother and child are bathed in a hormone that creates a sense of loving, a sense of euphoria and fearlessness. Women, in a monstrously huge expectation of the worst pain they'll ever experience in a lifetime, often move straight to the pain blockers which, I would guess, also would logically block the natural flow of oxytocin to mother and child. The love affair that naturally arises under oxytocin's intoxicating effects is cut short by the mother and child's drug addled haze. What is more, as stated by Jean Liedloff:

> "Today normal is adversarial. The baby arrives and has an innate expectation that it will be among trustworthy allies. That's not what happens. From the baby's point of view he or she feels like "they're not on my side."

I know that I've pointed to this before, but it bears repeating. This is the limbic petri dish where the dramas take a foothold and grow.

I'm crying and miserable and everything feels wrong.

No one is helping me out of this scary place.

I must not have a right to signal that I am stressed and frightened.

I must not be lovable enough, or someone would respond to my crying.

I must not be enough.

When we're feeling *not enough*, we need to be able to point to reasons why we don't feel *enough*. It's simply too difficult to get to the root of the 'something's wrong' belief stored in the limbic brain, so a scapegoat needs to be named to identify the uncomfortable feeling. And, I know I don't have to spell out the myriad ways which we project our discomfort 'out there'. It's even done on a national scale. All the hideous ethnic 'cleansings' are done, in the name of this lurking and subterranean foe. We're not feeding our families, so it must be *their* fault. Our country is in a huge financial deficit and it's because of them. They're making me miserable. They are the reason for all my hardship. She is the reason for my suffering. He is why I don't sleep at night.

Rajae (July 2011)

I was at the market yesterday getting stuff to eat when I saw a woman that looked remarkably like Rajita. Rajita was an 18 year old when I met her, in 1970, fresh from Argentina living in the cold of her first Swiss winter. We'd play endlessly given we were both away from our much warmer, and former, homes. Rajita was related, in a way I was never clear on, to the family with whom I stayed in Switzerland. She'd laugh with an infectious abandon at my mispronunciation of the word "zut". Pronouncing it, like an American, with the "oo" sound instead of the French "u" sound.

When I recently arrived, here in Switzerland, I was told that Rajita had had a rough time. Life *happened* to Rajita. Losses and hardships, since her having come to Switzerland, had marked her. Yet, she was living in the same town as I was now staying. And while bicycling around town, I'd often expect to see her. I often hoped to see her, never thinking for a minute that it had been 40 years and she might not have the slightest idea who I was. At the market yesterday, I stood opposite a woman, and presumably her daughter, that looked very much like I'd have imagined Rajita to look. We looked at each other and, self-consciously, I turned away. I saw them once again just outside the market, and thought better of asking her if she was Rajita. A good 20 minutes later, I saw the same two walking with their groceries along one of the pedestrian-only cobblestone streets.

"Rajita?" I managed to say without even thinking as I rode by them on my bicycle.

"No," she said. "But, my name is Rajae." She said, smiling broadly.

"Was your name Rajita 40 years ago?" I said, feeling sure it was her.

"No," she said. "I've always been Rajae."

"Sorry," I said.

"I was only 5 years old 40 years ago," she continued.

"I didn't mean to be insulting, but I knew a woman that looked a lot like you. I mean, I would imagine that she'd look like you after 40 years...I mean, I'm sorry."

"Was she Moroccan?" she asked, seeing I was uncomfortable and trying to set me at ease.

I got off my bike and we began talking. It was wonderful to just meet someone I didn't know in Switzerland. People tend to be a bit to themselves in Yverdon. She and her daughter were both smiling openly. I was feeling instantly and wonderfully comfortable with them.

"Actually, I don't know. I *do* know she had North African parents, but whether they were originally from Tunisia, Algeria, Morocco or even Lebanon, I never really knew." I said.

"You're on vacation here?" She asked.

"Yes. I'm American. I'm traveling with indefinite plans. I was in Australia for 5 months before coming to Europe..."

Her daughter, allowing her mother to drive the conversation because she was more of a contemporary of mine than she, suddenly spoke up.

"I was there for 8 months," Amanda announced.

"In Australia? Really?" I asked.

"Yes. I loved it..." Amanda continued.

The three of us spoke animatedly about Morocco, Switzerland and Australia. Pleased to have this unexpected encounter in the street, Rajae said she'd be pleased to have me over for dinner so we could talk some more. She felt that her husband and I would get along too.

~

Last night I went to their house for dinner. These two women I'd scarcely spoken to for 15 minutes had me over for dinner with a Moroccan meal with courses that kept coming. Olivier was French. And addressing the subject of innocence, he said, "Ever since I was very young, I've always been sure of two things:

It's simple.

I know.

Whereas I was intellectualizing about the two lobes of the brain and how innocence alludes us because of our incessant mentalizings, he calmly listened to me as I continued on and on enthusiastically. Then, when I had finished, he simply stated with perfect clarity what I've always known but never really tried to reduce to its utmost simplicity:

It's all simple and I already know.

We don't need to ask experts anything. We don't need to look to others for advice or approval. Probably the grandest of tricks, he felt, is that we are made to feel that it's all complicated. Sure it is. So we give it to someone else so they can take care of everything. We give it to our governments. We give it to the 'experts'. We give it to anyone even remotely suggesting that they know better than we. We give it away.

"Cats don't think about their lives; birds don't think about their lives," he said with a smile on his face. "They know. And, it's simple. We're on the cusp of living, as you say, more out of the right hemisphere of our brain. That's what this period of humankind is about: mentally bringing more stimulation to the right hemisphere of the brain," Olivier said as he looked to his step-daughter, Amanda.

"I don't know how to do it. I've wracked my brain how to do it, but I want to help get Amanda through school. I want to provide for my family. But, some really tricky guy has set it up that I can't just live 'simply and know'; I have to work. I have to get along with people that I don't always want to get along with. And that can be complicated," Olivier said.

I was genuinely surprised and pleased at how easily he allowed me into his family. He had none of the competitive-guy stuff going on. He saw me as a non-threatening stranger that fit effortlessly into his home and his sensibility.

"That's what I'm trying to figure out. I want to figure out how to stay in simplicity and simply exist without my having to make a living. I know it's possible," I said.

"But you're thinking about it...you see?" he insisted.

"But the mind isn't the bad guy. It's brilliantly equipped to help us. The very thing that complicates stuff for us can also simplify stuff for us." I said.

"Yes. We'll see," he said as he chewed thoughtfully at his food.

The evening went on like this. Rajae and Amanda as active in the conversation as Olivier, the four of us were fast realizing that we were all facing the same thing:

How to secure our basic natures amidst an impossibly crazy world while physical, mental and spiritual structures were falling down all around us.

An oasis, in a time of sequestering myself in front of my laptop, this was the break and touchstone I really needed. And, what a wonderful evening! Colorful and impassioned, our conversations were so very reminiscent of the late night discussions with Vladimir Vysotsky and many others.

Vientiane, Laos - 2011

CHAPTER 22

The Innocence of an Adult

THE LOGICAL SONG

R Davies, R Hodgson

When I was young
It seemed that life was so wonderful
A miracle, oh it was beautiful, magical
And all the birds in the trees
Well they'd be singing so happily
Joyfully, playfully watching me

But then they send me away
To teach me how to be sensible
Logical, responsible, practical
And then they showed me a world
Where I could be so dependable
Clinical, intellectual, cynical

There are times when all the world's asleep
The questions run too deep for such a simple man
Won't you please, please tell me what we've learned?
I know it sounds absurd but please tell me who I am ...

~

Sax player for Bruce Springsteen, RG Clemons, was once asked why he received almost as much applause as Springsteen on their shows together.

"It's because of my innocence," he said. "I have no agenda: just to be loved. Somebody said to me, 'Whenever somebody says your name, a smile comes to their face.' That's a great accolade. I strive to keep it that way."

I never hear much about adult innocence. Most of us would figure those words to be an oxymoron. In order for innocence to be an adult quality, certain shifts need to occur. And the changes need nearly be at the visceral, or cellular level. How on earth do we get there?

As pointed out in an earlier chapter, young children are able to see themselves as dancers, heroes, singers and scientists. They don't have room for, what's come to be called, "stinkin thinkin": Thoughts of not being good enough. The genius of the child is that they *know* when they're playing a game and they know when their imagination is creating a fanciful world. When their parents call them home, they know that they have to return to being a kid when they walk back in the house to sit down to dinner. The young girl knows it's time to leave her princess-self in the castle and have lunch. The young boy knows that he can slip out of his super-hero suit and return to being the child living in his parent's apartment above a parking garage.

As for us as adults:

We don't know that we're playing a game. We think it's all real. The job is real. The roles we play are real. The stress is real. And we don't know when or how to go home.

Where we fall down as adults, myself included, is that we don't realize that we've made this all up. We don't remember that we were bitten by the lizard to play his game. We play for real and for keeps and we get caught in the game, where a child would simply walk away from it; move to another game or go home and pretend being a kid. We believe that our stories and our beliefs are real such that they become the building blocks upon which we build a case for who we are.

In short, if the carefully laid bricks of cultural belief start to *shift*, the individual's cultural ego goes on alert as the "I am about to die" alarm is sounded. Because once the beliefs are questioned, it's over. The system is threatened with collapse because each belief is inextricably dependent on the next. It's like the consumer confidence index. The more comfortable people are with the way things are and how they are going, the stronger the market.

The most glaring example of this, for me, is when a deeply religious person resolutely states that the only way to God is through their respective religion. If that belief of theirs is challenged, more often than not, you've got an argument on your hands because they feel like you're telling them they're wrong. People with very fixed ideas of who they are and what they believe are well-defended and are even given to anger if the deeply cherished beliefs falter because of a probing question. People can so strongly identify themselves with their beliefs that challenging their world view can be seen as a threat to the very firmament upon which their *raison d'etre* is built.

Considered the father of astronomy, Galileo was among the first to discover mountains on the moon. For this and other discoveries like it, he came under harsh attack. When Galileo offered to have those disputing his discoveries to simply peer through his telescope to confirm it for themselves, *they refused*. Subsequently, Galileo was ordered to stand trial on suspicion of heresy in 1633 "for holding as true the false doctrine taught by some that the sun is the center of the world". The Roman Inquisition found him "vehemently suspect of heresy" and he was sentenced to life in prison. The sentence was based on literalist interpretations of Scripture[1]. Galileo was not formally vindicated by the Catholic Church until 1992![2]

This is an excellent historical example of the stubbornness with which we fight to uphold our beliefs so the whole pyramid of stories doesn't come toppling down. No stories – No "I". And how can we exist without an "I"?

When a world-view is challenged, a person committed to his beliefs that make up his world view, feels like he is under attack. He literally feels like the challenger is making an attempt on his life. And that attack is met in kind. This is the ground on which so many wars are fought. Why on earth would any war be fought on the grounds of opposing world-views or opposing religious beliefs? It's because it constitutes an attack on the collective ego that is weightily invested in its belief set. Simply: we have killed for our beliefs and we have died for our beliefs.

We don't even know we've made it all up. We're not even consciously aware that we *are* our beliefs. And, painfully, who pays for this?: children caught in

[1] Chronicles 16:30, Psalm 93:1,Psalm 96:10, Psalm 104:5, Ecclesiastes 1:5

[2] L'Osservatore Romano N. 44 (1264) - November 4, 1992

the cross-fire. In these wars fought in the name of religion, racial differences, ideological differences and perceived threats, often the truly innocent victims are the children. They, like the Afghan Girl, are victims of emotional trauma. Children are the collateral damage, yet again, of adult mismanagement.

Killing in the name of our beliefs!? Beliefs must be verrrrrrrrrrrry important to make such an important statement like: taking or giving up a life

The Innocent Adult

So how do we reformat the notion of the innocent adult so that it's not something that is regarded as being weak, wimpy, naïve, under-educated, virginal, childish or overly imaginative? There was certainly nothing about Clarence Clemons that was any of those things. His was a huge presence. A strong male presence, yet he felt that people liked him (loved him!) because of his innocence. His innocence! Not because of his strength or his power as a sax player. Not because of his imposing mass and the fact that he was a former college football player meant for a career with the Cleveland Browns. Not because he was rock and roll's Big Man. But, his *innocence.*

I just watched an interview with him recorded in 2009. For me, he struck me as having that wonderful "what-you-see-is-what-you-get" aura about him. Genuine. Loving. Candid. Huge-hearted. And he seemed to have an enormous ease in his own skin. This is the type of person most all of us enjoy being around. Because of his honesty and lack of pretense, there seems an unspoken invitation for us to step into the same place. And it's a place that knows no judgment, preconception, avarice, or malice. Personally, I knew very little of Clarence Clemens and his involvement in the E Street Band. I think he was called "Big Man" not because of his physical stature, but because he was a big man with*in* himself. He seemed to me to be the kind of person that looked squarely into the face of his own demons, doubts and insecurities and just decided that life was too short. It was too short to live in any other state but love. Living his own example, a welcome mat is laid out for everyone in his circle to do the same.

Adult Maturity's Next Step

Adult innocence is the 'next step' we can take in our own adult maturity. I believe it's the final frontier. I'd like to explain what I mean by that.

Everything, by simple virtue of the fact that we're speeding through space as a planet, solar system and galaxy, is subject to change. And life is in a dynamic, undulating and ever-changing state of flux.

What belief, story, hypothesis, postulate or notion can stand, unshaken, in the midst of change?

If **change** is the **wind**, which is stronger: the oak or the reed?

I am finding that the beliefs and stories I have about myself, while they appear to make me stronger, only weaken me as a person because they only engender inflexibility. If I have no beliefs to stand behind, the winds of change cannot challenge the image I have of myself. The more empty my vessel, the greater the ease with which I can weather the change. And this is of particular importance, now, in this time of unprecedented cultural upheaval and reassessment. And, personally, I feel we've merely seen the tip of the iceberg. I think our best insurance in seeing our way through the dramatic financial, social, structural and planetary changes ahead, is to *not* be so sure about what we believe to be true.

Everything that I have known myself to be identified with will own me, just like all my former possessions owned me. Nowhere has it become more obvious than in the world of today's home mortgages. Paying a mortgage on a home was the most savvy economic move we could make as baby boomers... that is until 2008 came along. Many of us have found ourselves quite literally being slaves to the very thing we once called our beloved one and only financial security. Our home was our nest egg. It was our own miniature bank from which we could pull out second mortgages and secured loans like an ATM machine. I did it too. We were encouraged to do it by our accountants, friends and family.

The mortgaged home, as an investment, was a rock-solid and unchallenged good choice for the future. It was a belief that was unseated, however, by the wily winds of change.

'I am a runner' is also a belief until I sprain my ankle and I am no longer a runner, for a while anyway. 'I am a wealthy man' is a belief until I lose everything in the stock market. 'I am an intelligent man', until I meet someone that I esteem to be far more intelligent than I. 'I am a vital young man', until my aging body tells me differently.

I could tell, just by watching Clarence Clemens speak, that he was unattached and dis-identified with his possessions, beliefs and stories. He was purely and comfortably in the moment. Enviably so.

This next step into adult maturity is something I believe can happen with all my heart, or I wouldn't have decided to write this book. The road is clear:

I need to see my self-identifications (everything I believe about myself) as Christmas ornaments on the Christmas tree, knowing that I am the tree and not its ornaments. I am the tree drinking up the sun from the sky and the water from the ground. The ornaments are hung on my branches until the howling winds of change come along.

The intuitive mind is a sacred gift

and the rational mind is a faithful servant

- Albert Einstein

~

BUT

We've allowed ourselves to create a society that respects and encourages the servant --

but has forgotten about the gift.

Bibra Lake, W. Australia

CHAPTER 23

Even God likes a Good Mystery

I KNOW ABSOLUTELY NOTHING. And the less I know, the freer I am. And the freer I am, the more I realize that life is the grandest of mysteries. Life is the grand dame of perplexities. It's unknowable, unfathomable, inconsistent, immeasurable, incomprehensible, undefinable, and for me it's beyond all I know and understand.

It is precisely the ineffability of creation and creativity that keeps wonder permanently a part of this cosmos. The wonder of creation itself is the quintessential magic. Because creation infers creating something from nothing. It's like 1+1 is 3. Two energies come together to create another one – separate and apart from themselves. Where did the other 1 come from? It was 'created'. Created from what? From where? Ah, the mystery of it. And you'll never learn that 1+1=3 in school – in quantum physics, maybe.

Ponder the Seed – Blow your Mind

A lone seed tumbles to the ground. It rains and the sun shines and out of nowhere: there's a pumpkin, or an apple tree, or a flower. How does this seed "know" what it is and what it is to become? What intelligence orchestrates this inordinately complex system of events in the creation of the pumpkin.

It's magic. And it's all around us. All the time. And it's nearly too mind-blowing to think about for too long.

A few people have asked me, "How did you write that song? Where did it come from?"

"Well," I say, "I wrote these words and then the words seemed to suggest a melody to me and, well, then I had a song..."

There it is: creativity seems to seduce substance out of the ether and most of us can't wrap our brains around that one.

Brahms, however, had a unique and altogether articulate way of describing his creative process:

> To realize that we are one with the Creator, as Beethoven did, is a wonderful and awe-inspiring experience. Very few human beings ever come into that realization and this is why there are so few great composers or creative geniuses in any line of human endeavor. I always contemplate all this before starting to compose. This is the first step. . . .
>
> I immediately feel vibrations that thrill my whole being. . . . In this exalted state, I see clearly what is obscure in my ordinary moods; then I feel capable of drawing inspiration from above, as Beethoven did. . . .
>
> Straightaway the ideas flow in upon me, and not only do I see distinct themes in my mind's eye, but they are clothed in the right forms, harmonies, and orchestrations. Measure by measure, the finished product is revealed to me when I am in those rare, inspired moods. . . . I have to be in a semi-trance condition to get such results — a condition when the conscious mind is in temporary abeyance and the sub-conscious is in control, for it is through the subconscious mind, which is part of Omnipotence, that the inspiration comes. I have to be careful, however, not to lose conscious-ness, otherwise the ideas fade away.
>
> [The term "subconscious"] is the most inappropriate name . . . super-conscious could be a much better term.

The real genius draws on the Infinite source of Wisdom and Power as Milton and Beethoven did. That is, in my opinion, the best definition of genius. . . . Great powers like Goethe, Schiller, Milton, Tennyson and Wordsworth received the Cosmic vibrations of eternal Truths because they linked themselves to the infinite energy of the Cosmos. . . .

The themes that will endure in my compositions all come to me in this way. It has always been such a wonderful experience. . . . I felt that I was, for the moment, in tune with the Infinite, and there is no thrill like it.[1]

The creative process speaks to the mystery of life itself.

My best guess is that, at some point in a person's life, this question is invariably addressed:

"What's all this about?"

or

D'Où Venons Nous/ Que Sommes Nous/ Où Allons nous?

--Paul Gaugin

(Where do we come from/What are we/Where are we going?)

I'm way ahead of the game, I figure, if I just let it be a mystery and not feel at all compelled, as we tend in the West, to categorize everything.

I loved it when Deepak Chopra, when talking about the obsessive western tendency to want to categorize and name illnesses, said *something* like:

...Don't think of it as cancer...give it another name...

We become prisoners of these categories – all in the name of making sense of the world around us. In doing so, we're trying to create order where there

---

[1] Arthur M. Abell, *Talks with Great Composers* (New York: Philosophical Library, (1955)

is none: systems where there never were, linearity where it doesn't belong, logic amidst what is most obviously illogical, and understanding where there can never hope to be.

If everything is changing. All the time. How can anything be frozen in a category when the firmament upon which we've relegated this category is, itself, changing?

And as long as there is mystery: there is inquiry, fascination, wonder and surprise. And that's why I believe God likes a good mystery. If everything is unknowable, that leaves LOTS of room for life itself to *breathe*. Life is free to be whatever it wants. And if God knew what was going on all the time, there would be no surprises. No new stories. Nothing new under the sun. Personally, I don't think God would have it any other way.

And nowhere is mystery more alive than in the child. When a child watches a bug or a bird or light splitting into a magnificent rainbow of color dancing around a room, there is wonder in everything. And it's all a big fat Greek mystery.

Why is the sky blue?

Why are there clouds?

Why do birds fly?

Why do the oceans have waves?

You've seen it. Children will ask questions incessantly. And every answer gives rise to 10 more questions. Why? Because they need to categorize the objects and events in their world? No. It's because everything is amazing and everything is a mystery and unknowable. OK. The sky is blue because the color blue has a shorter wavelength and is more easily absorbed by the gas molecules in the atmosphere. Then, the absorbed blue light gets scattered around the sky. This is not only wholly unsatisfying to me, but probably as mystifying and crazy-making to a child. The sky is blue because: It's amazing! That's why. Blue is a wondrous color and it's beautiful.

For one of the children's theme CDs I produced about our solar system, I asked children ages 4 and 5 to explain why stars twinkled. Here are some answers I got:

> When the moon shines the stars twinkle.

> The stars have points on them and they can move around.

They *have* to twinkle.

They're happy.

They twinkle because we love them.

They make the sky have a little bit of decoration so it will be pretty.

If you wanted to look at the stars and there were no stars you wouldn't be happy.

The above is an example in which the child's perspective allows for anything to be possible. They twinkle, basically, for whatever reason suits their fancy in the moment. The child sees this infinite and wondrous universe as something magical that interfaces with their personal world. My favorite response to the question?:

Stars twinkle because we love them.

☆

There are as many answers as there are stars in the sky, I'd guess.

Many of us take the night sky for granted. Carl Sagan didn't. All we have to do is watch Carl Sagan speak about this universe to know that the child within him was very much alive and that this child within him probably fueled most of his questions about the universe. And this is a universe that was made all the richer, for us, through his insatiable curiosity about the stars and beyond. And, I'd guess, that Carl would have been right up there with many children thinking that, on some level, stars twinkle... because we love them.

Indisputably, one of the greatest of scientists of the last century was humbled by the unknowable in spite of his vast understanding of the sciences when he stated:

> *"The most beautiful thing we can experience is the mysterious. It is the source of all true art and all science. He to whom this emotion is a stranger, who can no longer pause to wonder and stand rapt in awe, is as good as dead: his eyes are closed."*

-Albert Einstein

Well acquainted with the childlike sense of play, and humor, Einstein's ability to place himself in a childlike state of wonder and curiosity was the essence of his genius.

"There are two ways to live: you can live as if nothing is a miracle; you can live as if everything is a miracle."

-Albert Einstein

And there's this one:

"A knowledge of the existence of something we cannot penetrate, of the manifestations of the profoundest reason and the most radiant beauty, which are only accessible to our reason in their most elementary forms—it is this knowledge and this emotion that constitute the truly religious attitude; in this sense, and in this alone, I am a deeply religious man." [2]

-Albert Einstein

and then I asked an 8 year old why stars twinkle:

The atmosphere passes over the star and it makes them, kind of, flicker.

He had already removed him*self* from the stars twinkling equation and ventured a scientific explanation for the phenomenon. His world, some-where between the age of 4 and 8, began differentiating[3] and basically he separated his emotional involvement with a twinkling star and cast it out into the more responsible and scientific world of the classifiable. Whether he was trying to please his teacher, his parents or simply trying to do the right things, he gave away part of something so completely magical in his child-self. And, it happened virtually overnight -- with the bite of the lizard.

---

[2] Albert Einstein (1949) The World as I See it   New York Philosophical Library

[3] Differentiation is a term in system theory (found in sociology.) From the viewpoint of this theory, the principal feature of modern society is the increased process of system differentiation as a way of dealing with the complexity of its environment. This is accomplished through the creation of subsystems in an effort to copy within a system the difference between it and the environment. The differentiation process is a means of increasing the complexity of a system, since each subsystem can make different connections with other subsystems. - Wikipedia (Ritzer 2007:95-96).

Einstein, himself, seemed to me to have had a love-hate relationship with science. Mathematics was his refuge from the ordinariness of life. It had a purity within it for him. At age 26, he published his Theory of Relativity. Yet, nearly 40 years later, he saw how his theory of relativity was perverted by the military in the creation of the atomic bomb, and he was appalled when many saw him as being the father of the nuclear fusion. But more importantly, he saw science as being a mere part of the big picture and that, alone, it was limited.

"Imagination ... is more important than knowledge. Knowledge is limited. Imagination encircles the world."[4]

Science, according to my understanding anyway, is based on hypotheses, theories, assumptions and probabilities. But if a hypothesis is built on the already shifting sands of change and dissolution, down come tumbling the theorems, and statistical probabilities with it. (Somewhat like the Federal Reserve...only different)

Aristotle maintained in his definition of science:

...scientific knowledge is a body of reliable knowledge that can be logically and rationally explained.

How does innocence emerge from a world that is scientifically explained? Simple: it doesn't. But a scientific world view can be an important component nonetheless in the re-emergence of innocence in the adult.

Accepting science as a world view and as another way to explain the often unexplainable, doesn't necessarily mean that innocence cannot be a part of this perspective. Science simply needs to be regarded as another side in the many-faceted gem that is life. Period. Science is a beautiful and elegant way of quantifying the mysteries of life from an entirely and profoundly empirical perspective – from the perspective of the left brain.

[4] Viereck, George Sylvester (October 26, 1929). "What life means to Einstein: an interview". *The Saturday Evening Post*

Science becomes, quite simply, yet another wonder of life. After all, to be *totally* in the right brain as Jill Bolte Taylor's *Stroke of Insight* experience[5] would suggest, innocence and the wonder in which it is encased would have no ballast, no grounding and no frame of reference.

Being in a total state of wonder at the mystery of it all would decidedly have its pitfalls, that is, were it not for the "come-back-to-planet-earth" urgings of the ever-tabulating and ever-alert left lobe of the brain.

Wonder *can* live side-by-side with a logical and rational world view, can't it?

Wonder *should* live side-by-side with a logical world view. Together, they can make magic..

Living between these two worlds is where I've made my home for much of my life, and now it's time to get real with it. Now is the time to live between those two worlds without apology and without giving the slightest consideration...to leading a dual life. Why? Because living between the two worlds is rapidly becoming as natural and as effortless, for me now, as breathing.

~

It's a wonder why so few of us wonder about the wonder of it all.

---

[5] The neuro-anatomist and spokesperson for the Harvard Brain Tissue Resource Center who survived a stroke in 1996, at age 37, who described the shifts in her brain that took place as the left hemisphere was shutting down.

Black swans and their cygnets, W. Australia - 2012

Every moment of light and dark is a miracle.

-Walt Whitman

Yverdon-les-Bains at Lake Neuchatel - 2011

CHAPTER 24

Fluffifying the Cerebellum

"A mind that is stretched by a new experience can never go back to its old dimensions."

- Oliver Wendell Holmes, Jr.

I have long done some of the craziest things to guard against brain atrophy. It's been a big deal for me. Always. I learned juggling. I taught myself to play piano. I have been an active journal writer since my teens. I traveled a LOT. For several years recently, I'd had one hour sessions once a week of speaking French, German and Spanish with no transition time between each 20 minute interval. And, I've cycled through many professions including piano and voice teacher, SCUBA instructor, videographer, audio book narrator, playwright, music director, children's recording artist, animation and radio/TV voice-over actor, textile salesman and I'm sure I've left out a couple.

Though I have a pressing penchant for the comforts provided by a routine, on the other hand, I'm constantly trying to destabilize my brain so it is incapable of settling into anything that smacks of the predictable or humdrum. Sending those neurons careening down new pathways like mini adventurer explorers has often been my intent, conscious or unconscious. Personally, I feel the brain wants this. Needs this. In the same way that bone density is increased with weight-lifting (by pushing the limits); the heart and vascular system are made more healthy with exercise, the brain needs exercise for better 'file' access. And the exercise it needs is a fanning of neural firings over the greater part of the brain's 'lost territory'.

"Cognitive therapy is nothing more than learning the appropriate strategies, methods, and concepts so that our brains can change. Our new neural pathways continue to grow and our new feelings, beliefs, and thoughts changed automatically, too." [1]

The kind of neural firing I was looking to encourage was like shooting a cannon down a bowling alley. Removing myself from my environment in an attempt to erase how people knew me and who I was in the world...like going into the theater dressing room, backstage, and emerging as a totally different character. Or, if the brain were a computer, reformatting the hard drive.

Why? Because I could.

Not surprisingly, there have been numerous studies on this very topic:

'We challenged half of the volunteers to learn to do something entirely new. After six weeks of juggling training, we saw changes in the white matter of this group compared to the others who had received no training. The changes were in regions of the brain which are involved in reaching and grasping in the periphery of vision, so that seems to make a lot of sense. [2]

---

[1] Social Anxiety, Chemical Imbalances in the Brain, and Brain Neural Pathways and Associations: What Does It All Mean? Thomas A. Richards, Ph.D. _Psychologist/Director, SAI

[2] Oxford University study October 2009 - Jan Scholz

Near Augusta W. Australia - 2012

CHAPTER 25

The Duality Duel

HAVING TWO ENTIRELY different and opposing perspectives on our world as seen by each lobe of the brain isn't near the curse it might suggest. We're given the unique privilege of being able to actually witness the two of them operating independently of one another if we choose, and if we're really good observers. Using the analogy of the automobile to describe the way the two hemispheres of the brain operate: The right brain is the accelerator and the left brain is the brake. They work well together to keep everybody safe.

The dual human nature is referenced in the literature of most all religions:

> Jesus was half God and half Man.

> Shiva the Destroyer is also Shiva the Creator.

> God and Muhammad share equal importance though one is human and the other divine.

In religious study, particular attention is given to the harmonizing and, eventual unification of the dual aspects:

"When you make the two one, and when you make the inner
as the outer and the outer as the inner and the above as the
below and when you make the male and female into a single
one, so that the male will not be male and the female not be
female. Then you shall enter the Kingdom." [1]

The common line is the *unification and balancing* of the male and female; the
good and bad; the animal nature and the divine nature; balancing yin and
yang; alpha and the omega.

Personally, I see a link to this balancing of two opposites in the human brain:
The left hemisphere of the brain being data oriented and the right hemisphere of the brain being experience oriented and the corpus callosum's
appointed position to bring balance to them.

So, the left brain which sums up its world like an accountant's ledger is
softened by the more holistic perspective of the right brain. Without the all
important mediating third party, the corpus callosum, we have a runaway
brain working automatically with nary a word from the Lord and Master of
this mind/body kingdom: YOU.

The Artist – Primarily Right Brain-Influenced

The artist, whose creations generally come from a right dominated brain,
reminds us with his art of our softer nature. The artist reminds us why we're
alive. The artist reminds us that beauty exists among us. We need only notice
it.

Additionally, the artist helps to wake us up from the cultural trance with a
gentle, and occasionally not so gentle, tap on the shoulder. Sometimes
through music, paintings, film, theater or poetry, the artist keeps suggesting
that we get back to the essential of who we are irrespective of our cultural
influences. Beneath the cultural and societal biases, the artists direct us to a
oneness uniting us all through the universality of laughter, beauty, music and
art. And if the government finds the art controversial or counter to the
interests of the government, the artist is often silenced, persecuted or asked
to leave the country. Among those artists are:

---

[1] The Gnostic Apostle Thomas: Chapter 24

Ai Weiwei openly criticized his government (China) with his powerful art.

Charlie Chaplin expressed, in his films and publicly, his disapproval of hating communists.

Paul Klee was denounced by the NAZI government for his degenerate art.

John Lennon was long feared by the CIA and the US government for his anti war activism and political songs, had a deportation notice sent to his house...among other harassments.

The tortured artist has long been a cultural icon. Misunderstood, and alienated "due to the perceived ignorance or neglect of others who do not understand them and the things they feel are important." [2]

The following could be considered as well-known tortured artists:

Kurt Cobain

Marilyn Monroe

F. Scott Fitzgerald

Judy Garland

Vincent Van Gogh

Ernest Hemingway

Frida Kahlo

Oscar Wilde

I've met and known many artists in my life. Famous and not-so-famous. They all seem to have a very alive child inside of them. And the child lives there because they don't allow their vulnerability to be compromised. They *stay* vulnerable. As such, they *can* be easily hurt. But they would much rather risk being hurt than being invulnerable. Without their vulnerability, their artistic side doesn't seem to be able to express itself fully. Without their artistic side, they'd rather be dead.

---

[2] Wikipedia on the *Tortured Artist*

The Non-Artistic or Primarily Left Brain-Influenced

The non-artistic ones (if there's such a thing) are the worker bees – making sure planes fly, cars drive, governments work, TV and radio stations transmit and that the whole social machine works better and more effectively than it did before we got to it. The ultra-left brainers tend to be the statisticians, data collectors and technicians.

Together, the left-brain-dominant people and right-brain-dominant people make for an incredibly balanced society. And, ideally we'd like to have that incredible sense of balance within *us* as well – by balancing the left and right hemispheres of the brain. I think both lobes work to create the perfectly balanced psyche. They are the yin and the yang of a balanced perspective.

Me at a year old

CHAPTER 26

Innocence and the Right Brain

The development of functional brain asymmetry during childhood is confirmed by changes in cerebral blood flow measured at rest using dynamic single photon emission computed tomography. Between 1 and 3 years of age, the blood flow shows a right hemispheric predominance, mainly due to the activity in the posterior associative area.

Asymmetry shifts to the left after 3 years. The subsequent time course of changes appear to follow the emergence of functions localized initially on the right, but later on the left hemisphere (i.e. visuospatial and later language abilities). These findings support the hypothesis that, in man, the right hemisphere develops its functions earlier than the left.[1]

While the left brain sees and assesses its environment with words, based on the past and the future, the right brain processes only the present moment using the senses. It is no wonder, therefore, that a child seems innocent to us. The child is experiencing a kind of eternally-in-the-moment-overload

[1] Brain (1997), 120, 1057–1065 – C. Chiron, I. Jambaque, R. Nabbout, R. Lounes, A. Syrota and O. Dulac

because, for all intents and purposes, his world is undifferentiated and filled with truckloads of new input every minute. Everything is undulating around the child with uninterrupted fluidity. And that innocence continues until the slow but inexorable shift begins around age three. Traces of that innocence remain into childhood until the "I am" asserts itself so proudly, that the right brain backs off. The "I am" awareness eclipses the experiential right lobe awareness using words that define, separate and categorize. As Jill Bolte Taylor described in her experience[2] of the stroke she had in the left hemisphere of her brain (which led to the shutting down of that left hemisphere), she didn't know where her arm left off and the wall began. She was experiencing the moment without actually processing it.

Meditators claim meditation to be a profoundly right brain activity. It calms the left brain's chatter and stills our, at times, obsessive relationship to 'doing'. East Indian mystics often exhibit behaviors suggesting an altered or rapturous state of being that would point to their awareness being on the 'outside' of a commonly accepted world-view.

Innocence could be said to live here. Here in the right brain. Here where absent-minded professors lose track of time. Here, where artists forget to eat and sleep. Here, where inventors forget who they are. Here, as Brahms claimed he was:

"...in tune with the Infinite, and there is no thrill like it."

As adults living uniquely in the right brain, we couldn't reasonably be expected to hang the laundry, pay bills, go to our sister's birthday party, or talk to a bunch of our friends without acting like we're on LSD. The right brain allows no space between *us* – and everything *else*. We'd be one big happy molecular-ly interlacing family (which we are anyway...but, more about that later).

The left brain needs to help us process information and steer our motor skills to actually hang the laundry. Where I have watched myself get stuck for example, is in allowing the left brain to run off on its own and take over. It will run the whole show. If I let it. And I have let it do that often enough.

---

2 *My Stroke of Insight* – Jill Bolte Taylor, Hodder Paperback

Enter Corpus Callosum

The corpus callosum is the neutral witness and mediator. It is the referee that attempts to keep the two worlds balanced by delivering messages between the two hemispheres. Brokering and translating information, it uses roughly 200-300 million contralateral axonal fibres to bridge the gap between lobes. It decides which lobe is up to the task at hand. If an analytical, logical or rational perspective is needed, the task is issued to the left brain. If a more random, holistic or intuitive processing is needed, the information is forwarded to the right brain. In the most basic sense, it's a type of mail-sorter.

But who or what is behind the corpus callosum and its ability to decide which of these hemispheres is dominant when the issue is outside the domain of motor skills and simple tasks?

This is where I might be going out on a limb:

I think our volition conducts the non-automated functions of the corpus callosum. It is within our ability to orchestrate how the two lobes of the brain relate to one another. We are able, if we choose, to direct the corpus callosum to deliver informational and sensory input to the one lobe or the other to, ultimately, select the perspective from which we will process the input: from our imaginative center or our analytical center.

Our will is probably what underscores our divine nature. With our will we can create. With our will we can set intentions that have the power to seduce manifestation out of apparent nothingness. The will is the space between the two hemispheres. And the corpus callosum could be said to be the seat of our volition.

If two opposites co-exist in a system and a third "neutral" component organizes them, we have a trinity re-mindful of so many others:

Body, Mind and Soul

Past, Future and Present

Father, Mother, God

Positive, Negative, Neutral

Father, Son and the Holy Spirit

Brahma, Vishnu and Shiva

Birth, Death and Life

Day, Night and Twilight (or dusk)

The Space Between Worlds

For me, this is where this near two years of travel (so far), stuff divestiture and reflection have led me: To the archetypal importance of the triad and how the convergence of two energies creates a third energy. I had no idea this would have any importance in my own journey toward innocence but it did and this is what became clear to me. First, let me back up a little:

Maya, my house-mate at the time, in 1994, was scheduled to attend a workshop in Assisi, Italy that dealt with the relationship between psychotherapy and, of all things, quantum physics. We'd fallen in love a few months before the week workshop in Italy and, in an absolutely stunning move on my part, I suggested we both get married as long as we were in Italy (the country of my maternal grandparents). While we *did* get married in Assisi, the workshop fascinated me endlessly. From my perspective anyway, central to the week was the research of David Bohm. David Bohm, wrote exquisitely on how the particles in a field behave.

At the risk of over-simplifying what I remember to have been an exhaustively well written posit on particle theory, I'll summarize:

If a particle in a unified field is moving randomly, the introduction of a 2nd particle creates a tension (or, an 'awareness' of the other) as that 2nd particle becomes the 1st particle's opposite. From this tension arises a 3rd energy: A transcendent or reconciling 3rd energy. This 3rd energy has a harmonizing and solidifying influence on the two originally opposite energies. Whew! Heady, but amazingly simple at the same time.

In the context of the workshop in Assisi, this quantum physical model was used to explain the third energy arising in a therapist-client relationship. As such, the therapist has an equal amount to learn from the client as the other way around. It is essentially the energy that is created when two people come together in ANY relationship. A third energy appears as the result of the convergence of two. One plus one equals...three!

The hauntingly familiar notion of the archetypal triad is expressed throughout recorded history. If the Hindus for example see this life, we experience, as one of duality: pleasure/pain etc., there *must* be a third energy which can free us from the dualistic illusion of hot/cold – good/bad.

~

Everyone is a hero. This is a given.

We have a call to adventure.

We refuse.

A crisis ensues.

We cannot turn back-and we answer the call.

We collect helpers, teachers, guides.

And we cross the threshold into the unknown.

We lose our identity and enter an abyss, a nadir, the belly of a whale.

We emerge.

We begin traveling back home to what we have known-

re-crossing the threshold.

We return.

We have changed.

Joseph Campbell The Hero with a Thousand Faces (1949)

This third energy emerges as neither right or wrong; good or bad. It is the energy on the seam of opposites. Film makers and photographers speak often of the "magic" or "golden hour" of dusk. It's a magical time between day and night. How often have you had the impression that anything was possible at dusk? Ask any kid, – you can run, bicycle or fly much faster at dusk. It's simply conventional kid-wisdom. The Greek mythological figure Horus succumbs to Seth in this brief hour when neither of the gods are all powerful. Their power shifts from one to the other. At that sacred time, eternity exists between the light of day and dark of night.

And here is where I return to the idea of the door, the veil, the passage... the space between worlds. It is by way of this third energy; this transcendent energy, where we can claim our birth right and where the genius of the will can be employed to make out of each of us, a hero.

I believe that we came here to move beyond the maddening vicissitudes and duality of Maya and to *awaken* the 3rd transcendent energy: the third eye, the mystical 'other'...the twilight between day and night – the magical power between the respective reigns of Horus (day) and Seth (night).

Innocence's home is in the vulnerable, the belief-less. It is between the two worlds creating a third world. And it's ours for the taking. The stage simply needs to be swept clean of supposition and the insistent nay-saying and nervous finger-tapping of the left brain.

A classical example of the emerging 3rd energy is in sacred geometry's vesica piscis. Two circles move together bringing the outside edge of each to the midway point of the other to form this sacred space.

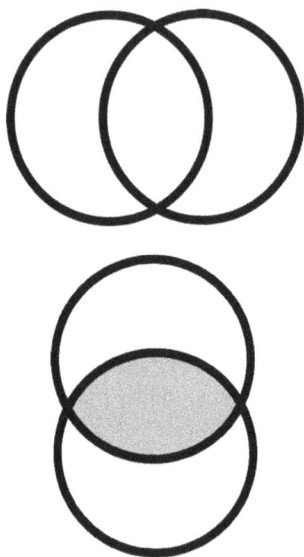

This vesica piscis, ubiquitous throughout sacred geometry, is known as the womb of the universe. It also looks like the all-seeing single eye.

.. if therefore thine eye be single, thy whole body shall be full of light

- Matt 6:22

And, its shape, appears everywhere in nature. If this shape could be viewed as the yoni, a womb and a single eye, something terrifically interesting emerges:

Within this sacred geometrical space is a world of non-duality, impartiality and purity. The space is non-dualistic, because it is the result of opposites recognizing each other and producing a transcendent third and non-local intelligent energy. Impartial, because it doesn't belong to a world of duality. Pure, because it stands as the unsullied observer of two opposing worlds.

From the trans-personal awareness within the womb, we slowly differentiate the world around us into all the qualities of duality we know so well as we become adults. And for those of us wanting more than to accept the conventionality of a dual universe, we try getting back to the womb of the single eye for the rest of our lives. Within the space between worlds, there is no joy that can be eclipsed by sorrow and there is no radiant health that can be crushed by disease. There is only the silent, abiding wonder that observes and experiences everything without being inside duality's drama.

Ancient cultures viewed the sex act as a sacred union where two individuals were privileged with the opportunity to increase their own trans-personal awareness as the coming together created a space between. Merging their awareness in the space between, they could sling shot each other through the veil to a world of expansion and ecstasy by channeling the sexual energy.

In ancient times, the soundest insurance for the survivability of the species was to create babies that were born into this love and expansion sponsored awareness. This was considered a great and worthy achievement. And though that mystical and transcendent experience is still available to us through conscious love-making, the importance of it has been diluted in recent times.

The 3 Portals

1   Immediately prior to the moment of orgasm, ocytocin (the love hormone) floods the body of the male and female – filling us with a powerful sense of love, fearlessness and rightness. Conscious love-making has long been known to be a portal to the transcendent other. The yonic vesica piscis

is the portal of the sacred union. In a physical sense, love-making can quite literally produce an*other*. A baby. From an energetic view, love-making can produce the transcendent *other* - opening a window long revered by the ancients and depicted in sacred sex representations in India and Egypt. The Tantric ideas spread far outside of India into Tibet, Nepal, China, Japan, Cambodia, Vietnam, and Indonesia offering the possibility that even house-holders could aspire to spiritual liberation -- not just monks. Tantra spiritual practices make available to the householder freedom from ignorance. It's no wonder that the sex act is often associated with mystical experiences and 'the earth moving'. On a grosser level, it's no wonder that sex is dangled tantalizingly in front of us in absolutely every corner of our lives – because it sells. I think, underneath the obvious draw sex has on us, is an even greater, yet unconscious desire, to be between worlds – in the rapturous momentary place of no stress, worry or attachment – the sacred place where duality doesn't exist. These orgasms are ours. They are the sacred moments in time, where there is no time. A part of us realizes that they're desirable, special and separate from the mundane. We're not taxed for them, we don't pay for them, and for many people around the world, it's quite simply the only entertainment that is readily available and free. To allow sex to transport us beyond its entertainment value, is to lay claim to the non-local; the transcendent experience of 'other'.

2   When a baby makes its way down the birth canal, the mother's brain produces enough ocytocin for herself and her child to enjoy, what can hopefully be, a painless and extraordinarily bonding experience. As well, it sets the stage for a torrid and dizzyingly euphoric love-affair between mother and child...just like that produced during the male/female union at the moment of orgasm. I feel sure that in the same way that we, in the west, are made nervous by the unknown, we interrupt this sacred birth event by separating mother from the child in these crucial minutes and hours after birth in an effort to control this mystical event keeping mother and child "safe". Birth is one of those wondrous, mystifyingly impossible events that we still can't fathom. And I know that every time I witness a birth, I am still transfixed at the miracle of it. Because, not unlike being with someone at the time of their death, birth allows us to witness a being passing from one world into another. And we just can't help ourselves. We're in awe of the portal every time it makes an appearance in our lives. I think we're fascinated by the wonder and the incomprehensibility of it.

3   Based on innumerable reports of those having experienced the ecstasy and expanded awareness in near death experiences, I'd guess the brain

must produce its last gasp of oxytocin to free a person from his body thus making the transition euphoric. The long tunnel and blinding white light and the loving/non-judgmental presence at the time of death has made its way into common knowledge. A Gallup poll suggests that "approximately 8 million Americans" have experienced near-death experiences[3] or NDE's. With recorded reports of the after-life dating back to the 4th century BC, even Wikipedia offers this description, among many others, as typical of the NDE experience:

> A sense of peace, well-being and painlessness. Positive emotions. A feeling of being removed from the world. [4]

> Many view the NDE as the precursor to an afterlife experience, claiming that the NDE cannot be adequately explained by physiological or psychological causes, and that the phenomenon conclusively demonstrates that human consciousness can function independently of brain activity.[5]

Those assisting someone while they pass over, have similarly reported anomalous and unexplainable changes in the person as they approach their death. Even the elderly as they draw toward the closing of their lives, seem to become more innocent. With not a thought for fitting in, they are careening for the exit where they don't need to be socialized any more. They drop their social vestment as they approach their only real solitary journey (other than birth). The entry, like the exit, is made alone. The closer we are to the portals of birth and death, the closer we seem to be to this state of pure awareness. Everything in between (our lives as we know them) emerges as the tricky part.

It seems like the portal stays open briefly then, like the iris on a camera, it closes. I sensed the opening in the veil with every inch of my being and I knew I could walk through when my wife died. No one could have ever told me differently. Even to this day.

---

[3] Mauro, James "Bright lights, big mystery". *Psychology Today*, July 1992.

[4] Mauro, James. "Bright lights, big mystery", *Psychology Today*, July 1992. – van Lommel P, van Wees R, Meyers V, Elfferich I. (2001) "Near-Death Experience in Survivors of Cardiac Arrest: A prospective Study in the Netherlands," *The Lancet*, December 15; 358 (9298):2039-45. Near-Death Experiences: Is this what happens when we die? Durham: International Association for Near-Death Studies

[5] Rivas T. (2003). "The Survivalist Interpretation of Recent Studies into the Near-Death Experience." Journal of Religion and Psychical Research, 26, 1, 27-31

These are the three portholes. These are the doorways experienced at birth, during love-making and at death. Ocytocin is the lubricant used to shepherd us over the veil. And, irrespective of whether it's the "love hormone" or Kool-Aid, the body, mind and soul have an intimate and time-honored awareness of this gateway because this triumvirate mind, body, soul has been doing it for longer than any of us know. And each of us seem to have an ancient respect and an awareness of this fleeting opening in the veil. It's like the dragonfly dancing hypnotically above our heads.

For me, the journey back to innocence has led me here. Here, where duality is only something that is witnessed and not participated in. Here, in the space between worlds where there is no judgment, no beliefs, no qualities of right and wrong and no opposites. Here, in the vesica piscis. I can tell you, this is not what I expected to discover. But, at the same time, it's also something that I've loved and longed for all of my life. Every time I'm writing a song, I go there. It's the softest and sweetest of places. On rare occasion, even in meditation it's there. And, in some profoundly compelling way, it's the most familiar thing in my life. What is more:

It's simple

and, I know

What do the portholes have to do with innocence? Infants, prior to age four, and the elderly, before passing, seem to be most innocent. The elderly, with more time on their hands, appear to move into a state of child-like awe all over again when they regard the beauty of a flower. They will watch the vastness of the ocean with the same awe-inspired wonder of a child. It has most unequivocally appeared to me that the closer we are to either birth or death on our life's time-line, the more innocent we are.

For the child who hasn't yet been socialized, innocence expresses itself freely. The accrual of stress, loss, grief and trauma build and distract the child from being able to actually constellate his world against a backdrop of wonder. For the elderly, looking squarely in the face of their own mortality, whatever grief or stress that may have formerly been in their lives, falls away in importance as the incipience of their transition becomes more of a reality.

Of course there's that classic story of the 3 year-old girl who asks her parents if she can be alone with her barely 3-day old baby brother. Apprehensively they allow her to shut the door in the baby's room so she can speak with the new born in private. Over the baby-monitoring system they hear their daughter as she addresses her new baby brother: "Tell me about God, I've almost forgotten."

From porthole to porthole, we come in innocent and go out innocent. Somehow, though, we are distracted enough in between to forget about the wonder we came in with and, doubtless, will go out with.

The fetus transitions from not breathing to its first breath at birth. We transition, leaving our bodies behind, with our last breath. It is no wonder that the Eastern disciplines place so much emphasis on the breath: Because life is breath. And our relationship to ourselves is codified in the breath. In many Eastern practices, the most exalted attainment is that of the breathless state. This would be where all the autonomic physical responses come to a full stop. Because the mind and its duties are suspended, awareness is all there is: The Space Between.

This is where the vesica piscis becomes the cradle of innocence in the space between worlds.

Waking up this morning, I smile,
Twenty four brand new hours are before me.
I vow to live fully in each moment
and to look at all beings with eyes of compassion.

-Thich Nhat Hanh

Just trying to get along with each other, we tend to fumble like aliens on an alien planet -- at least, in the West. Indigenous peoples would probably say, of those of us in the West, that we'd lost our way and that in fearing death, we fear life. We just don't know what to make of birth and death. We're probably flummoxed by it all because we've become so estranged from the ways of nature. We no longer hear the voices of the animal spirits as the Native Americans did. All the pagan rituals having to do with the sun, moon and nature have been swallowed up and re-framed by the various religions...further separating us from our, at once, mysterious and natural relationship with nature.

CHAPTER 27

Bad Habits

I THINK THAT TO broker a shift in a life-style or a world-view is simply a matter of changing habits of belief. Habits, reinforced over a lifetime and encouraged by our culture, die hard. Our culture doesn't help us when it is constantly whispering post-hypnotic suggestions to keep those bad habits of thinking alive through our media. I've heard that the mindful practice of a new discipline can become a permanent part of a routine if it is practiced for 21-30 days. Similarly, *un*installing a bad habit takes 21-30 days to make it permanent.

Habits of erroneous thinking have kept me locked out of my own innocence. I will habitually defer to the findings of experts and statisticians over the voice of my intuition. Continuing to do this, I've only set myself up as a victim – a victim of forces outside myself. Victim consciousness is a habit just as the various forms of self-effacement are habits. If our lives were to reflect, as RG Clemons says earlier in the book, "...no agenda: just to be loved," that would mean a lot of beliefs would have to be eliminated and/or replaced by positive ones. Negative beliefs like:

I can't really trust anyone

I am not lovable

I am not enough.

What will they think when they find out I'm a fake?

In my experience, if I'm being distracted by day-to-to day survival and the stress that it entails, a part of my will gets left behind. And if I am not actively exerting my will or directing my thoughts, the task oriented nature of the left brain takes over. Its job is to protect me. But if it's using only information from the past and what it projects into the future, I can end up going somewhere I don't want to.

My dog, Allegro (non troppo), got along with everyone. He was always happy to see a stranger because it was an open invitation to either play or escape out of the house. And he loved them all: the neighbors, the mailman, the Mormons, the Jehovah's Witnesses and whomever else the day would throw at the front door when I lived in Southern California. With a knock at the door a Latino man, who I'd later get to know, like, respect, and employ, introduced himself to me as a gardener in the neighborhood. Allegro went nuts. He barked like he was staring at the face of the devil himself. And he barred teeth I didn't even know he had.

My only explanation?: Before I got him, as a puppy, he'd had a bad experience with someone holding a weed-wacker very much like this hapless gardener fellow standing at my door.

If I extrapolate this into my own life, people and places that remind me of experiences that were less than pleasurable are going to be judged and avoided. But that's just the left brain doing its job of protecting me. Based on past experience, and not wanting to repeat a bad experience, my left brain leaps to its command post and performs a job well done: I'll judge this person so I'll have nothing more to do with them. Great job.

Hey, but wait a minute. What if that person has *nothing* to do with the one that harmed me in the past? That would most certainly be a computational error and I could be selling myself short with what could otherwise be a great relationship. That error would not serve me. Just as it did not serve me when I judged this pirate-looking guy at the gym and he ended up being my best friend.

This is where the left brain needs to be informed, because my volition is in control. And a thoughtfully delivered message needs to be delivered to the left brain:

> You've done and are doing a great job here, Lefty, but I'm going to override your impulse to protect me and we're going to hand this job over to Righty so we can have a more expanded view on the situation.

This is called undoing a habit. The left brain has been allowed, by my lax observer, to control things. Habits are what keep me from accessing the holistic perspective of the right brain. And all the while Lefty thinks he's keeping me safe. And he's doing a damn good job of it. He's also keeping me from experiencing anything NEW. Because he is the one telling me:

> You've done that before
>
> You know this kind of person
>
> You've been to Cleveland before, you don't need to go again. (bad example)
>
> You've been in a relationship before and you got hurt. You don't need to do it again. (good example)
>
> Etc.

Simply put, I can get erroneous information from my ever diligent, and forever processing, left brain unless I deliberately stop the process. The way I stop the process is by summoning my will (by way of "the decider" – the Corpus Callosum).

Fortunately for me I've never had an addiction with, or even a taste for, smoking or drinking. I say, 'fortunately' because they're probably rough addictions to break and I'm somewhat of an addictive personality. My addictions showed up in other ways. And like for many of us these other addictions, because they're not as obvious, are far harder to notice or track. For me, I had and still have addictions to negative thoughts. On some level, I have found a perverse kind of comfort in them. I may lose all my friends but I'll always have my core beliefs and no one can take them from me. They are the beliefs of 'not enough'.

These are killers to deal with because they interlace seamlessly with a myriad of other beliefs and habits of bad thinking.

I'm not intelligent or caring enough

I don't make enough money

I'm no longer attractive to the opposite sex

I was fired because I'm not worth anything

I'm too old

These examples of "stinkin' thinkin'" erode our basic nature. And innocence IS our basic nature – our only real nature.

For me, several prominent conventions in the society, into which I was born, do a damn good job at keeping these bad habits of self-destructive thinking locked into this 'so-called' personality.

I rarely if ever watch TV. Not because I'm a snob. Not because I don't have one. But because I just end up not watching it. When I used to work out at the local gym, the bank of TVs plastered across the wall would strobe images from all the major TV networks. If my eye caught some inviting flash from the TV and I was drawn in, I noticed a few things happening to me while watching a program. I felt like I was undeserving and I felt unimportant. It was subtle. I didn't always notice it, but it was there. People on TV, particularly the morning "news" shows when I worked out, were pretty. They were happy. And they seemed to know a lot of stuff. They were aware of more stuff than I would guess I'd ever be. They were perfectly adapted to society. They were pitchmen for the societal trance.

> 'These are the bad things happening in the world today. Back to you, Katie"

> "Good news for cancer sufferers. Researchers are now saying that chocolate and coffee are good for you. That's right. They used to be bad for you, now experts say they're good." (etc.)

At the gym, I was not pretty (particularly in the morning). I was often stressed. I wasn't always happy. And, I wasn't much sure of anything.

Then came the commercial break with ads for:

> Depression medication

Erectile dysfunction

Sleeping aids

Deodorants

Pain medication

THAT's why I'm not like the happy. I need to buy all these *things* to make me 'right'.

While I don't really think this way now nor did I then, it's tempting. And the television with its programming and ad campaigns simply billboards each and every bad habit of belief we have about ourselves.

I'd even go so far as to say that my bad thought habits have helped to keep me hypnotized in the cultural matrix. And like Neo[1], I had to disconnect. I had to pull all the hoses off and endure the initial disorientation.

Undoing Bad Habits of Belief

I was shown a very simple and surprisingly effective way to deconstruct bad habits of belief. Let's take an example of:

"I'm not good enough"

Simply take the statement and turn it into a question and put the accent on a different word each time you repeat the question:

"*I'm* not good enough?"

"I'm *not* good enough?"

"I'm not *good* enough?"

"I'm not good *enough?*"

With these repetitions the brain begins to catch on that the belief was placed in your garden of beliefs...erroneously. That it was simply a mistake. A bad habit. And this belief, allowed to grow, becomes a weed that takes over your innocence garden. *The is one of the ways we can build a case against a destructive belief.*

---

[1] Neo was the central character in the film *THE MATRIX* (1999).

~

If I'm enslaved from within, I can be enslaved from without.

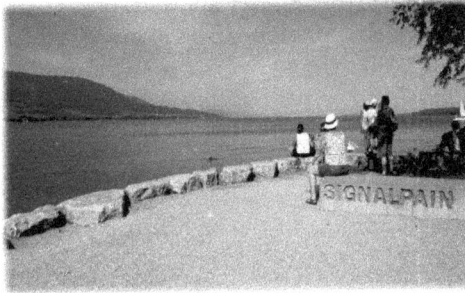

Yverdon-les-Bains, Switzerland - 2011

CHAPTER 28

Un-crazying Myself from the Pain of the World

A GURU CHALLENGED HIS disciple to meditate and not think of monkeys. Needless to say the disciple, while meditating, thought obsessively of each and every different type of monkey that he knew of.

Play, Laughter and Tears

We watch a puppy or kitten as they are constantly processing information of the world around them. In one vast discovery playground, they cycle between joy, frustration, play, anger and curiosity. These are not thoughts. These are the various states they are feeling and moving through -- one by one. As such, these myriad states are often ecstatic, but always pure, experiences because they are being lived experientially. They are not being considered or thought about. They are not wondering, "Hmmm, have I done this before?" The world in every shade of miracle is tumbling around them. And that's why we are helpless to love a puppy or a kitten. Because they are innocent. Isn't there a part of us that wants what they have? -- The ability to revel at the wonder of the world around them. Not to be romping around like kittens stalking each other and lunging sideways with arched backs, necessarily, but we DO want the ability to play without having a thought of feeling foolish. Because we know, instinctively, that play is where we rightfully live. I feel that innocence lives in play, laughter and in our tears. When I'm crying, whether from joy or sorrow, the last thing I'm thinking about is: Do I fit in or am I enough? When we're playing, laughing or crying, the tug from our beliefs releases its hold on us. They are the moments that we take for ourselves to be outside of our 'reality-adjusted' stresses and obligations. This is a space we clear just for ourselves. Here is where we skirt the space between the worlds of waking and sleeping where there are no thoughts – only feeling.

The tremendous relief I feel when I laugh is like being showered by a refreshing rain. It's as if the laughter shakes loose all the stress leaches that have attached themselves to me. The laughter quakes the walls and structures of my conditioning and sends them toppling down. And, the laughter gives me a reprieve from who I think I am. Ah...to be free and light like that all the time. There's a wonderful verb in French that has no direct translation in English: *se défouler.* I love this verb because it means to: un-crazy yourself. Have you ever felt you needed to shake off the craziness in you: To scream, or run, or yell obscenities, or dance until you can't dance anymore? I love this idea and it's the perfect antidote for a condition characterized in another of my favorite German words: *Weltschmerz* (The pain of the world). We can, and often do, un-crazy ourselves from the pain of the world. We do it using one of the many mini-portals. Playing, laughing and crying.

During times of social crises people tend to be far more inclined to want to be entertained and to laugh than at other times. They need to *se défoulent* (un-crazy themselves). Motion picture historians credit the year 1939 as being "The greatest year in the history of Hollywood movie-making" yet America stood on the brink of war. Bob Hope made history of bringing laughter to millions of US soldiers through four wars.

Many of the most interesting people I've met, including my wife, have been alcoholics. Their private *Weltschmerz* is so great, for many of them, that the numbing effects of alcohol are a choice that works for them...that is, until they are no longer under the effects of the alcohol. It's the same for drug-users. Those that I have known have been among the most sensitive people I've met. But their alcohol or drug deliverance from the heart-ache and the nastiness of "the things that happen" ends up being yet another problem...as well as a problem for those that care about them.

So how is innocence *possible* amid "the things that happen" in life?

CHAPTER 29

The Innocence of Children

EVERYWHERE IN ART and literature, we see examples of the adult wanting to be innocent once again, yet history bears out the perverse predilection humans have had to abuse the very children that embody this innocence. Indications that child abuse was, and still is, very much a part of nearly every society and culture points to this unaccountable split in our nature. The abuse is seen as disciplinary actions, child-labor, child slavery, or as emotional, physical and sexual abuse.

The mere mention of the treasonous act of an adult using a child's trust for their own gain, incites a torrent of anger, tears and disgust. Everyone now seems sensitive to the treatment of children. We love them, but history shows us that we have treated them like second class citizens... used as possessions, chattel, slaves and worse.

From the factual or mythical children's crusades of the early 13th century to today's sweatshops and child labor, we are constantly and uncomfortably reminded of this duplicity in our nature.

We tell them we love them, yet we hand them an unbelievably messy world to clean-up.

The *little* abuses can often go entirely under the radar when they ask for example:

"Are you OK, Dad?"

"Me? I'm... I'm fine."

"It seems like something's the matter," the child persists.

"Really, I'm fine."

This cuts them off from their own knowing. We can deny their intuition, without even being aware of it, when we try to protect them from the truth. And from the adult's point of view, this is totally understandable to want to protect them. We don't want to overly complicate their lives with our concerns. We want to keep it simple for them. But, children live in a feeling world and to deny them their feelings, is to cut them off from themselves.

We tell them we love them but tell them that faeries and their imaginary friends exist only in their imaginations.

We tell them we love them but, I discovered, many of them felt betrayed by adults because of the ruptured world we're handing them to make better.

We did try. We did. And, we did an *incredible* job of it.

Then, we got busy.

CHAPTER 30

Innocence

AND HERE I was. An adult. Unable to, finally, reconcile my own 'adultness' with an essential distrust of the adult nature. Did that mean that I correspondingly distrusted myself? Was there a traitor living in my own camp?

With the Peter Pan syndrome being barely an option, it was a conundrum at best. There had to be a way to incorporate the revered qualities of the child without actually trying to be an unattractive middle-aged Peter Pan. There can be few things more unappealing than an adult trying to *act* like a child. In movies, we're entertained by it and it can be very funny (Jerry Lewis, Lucille Ball, Pee Wee Herman, Tom Hanks in *Big*, Jim Carrey etc..); once outside of a Hollywood sound stage, however, you're likely to be institutionalized.

Mistakes

There were, doubtless, many mistakes we all made. And I have absolutely no hope at even getting a glimpse of my own innocence without being able to fully see my parents and their parents (and right on down the line) as the innocents they were. When I do see my parents as the innocent children they were before being subverted by the "things that happen in life", I can only love them more. When I consider all that doubtless happened in their lives and I really step into *their* shoes, they did a phenomenal job. (They did a phenomenal job anyway. Add to that, they are exceptional people as well.) Every inch of the way, they thought, *I* thought, *we* thought we were doing all the right things. Faithfully, and with the purest intent, we were trying to be good people and trying to make ourselves lovable. But without the grass-roots-knowing that we *are* good people and we *are* lovable when we begin life here, we fight to earn these badges of acceptability and it's the fight that derails us. It's the struggle for acceptance that, itself, perverts our best intentions.

And sure, there were all kinds of mistakes and bad choices I made. There are thousands of mistakes our culture has made. Because of our inextricably human foibles and because we live in a society that hasn't quite yet happened on a formula for the nurturing of infants and children, "mistakes" are written into the recipe of our culture. With our best intentions, we drift down the river of social influences and demands after childhood. Because of the effects were left with from an assembly-line-like main stream educational system, there is an un-doing that is necessary to be made on the personal level in order to become an honestly communicating and feeling human being. I don't think that there is any particular short cut.

We need to see this cultural machine as an *influence* in our lives and not the last word on who we are. The often spurious 'information' that comes flying down our media pipelines on radio and TV; in magazines; on billboards; in the news – these are the last gasps of a dying social order.

As long as the themes of 'not-enough' or 'something's wrong with me' are running, we're fair game for virtually any kind of manipulation or social machinery that, in most all cases, is not thinking about our well-being. We need to reclaim our relationships with each other; our relationship with the earth; our relationship with ourselves and not allow our self-concept to be eroded by the cultural storm of not-enoughness. Instead, we can create our own culture: a culture of 'enough'. We can write our own ticket and not accept someone else's worn out and no longer serviceable dream of a culture.

On the back of my sweatshirt from John Denver's Windstar Symposia was printed:

Never doubt that a small group of thoughtful, committed citizens can change the world. Indeed, it is the only thing that ever has.

-Margaret Mead

My guess?:

With the innocence of a child, we can dream another dream of what a culture is. We can sing a new world into existence in the same way we heard our mother's voice singing to us in the womb as she spoke. There is this huge power in voices singing united with an intention to change. We cannot listen to a choir singing passionately about something and not be moved. It's just plain impossible.

We can dream another culture using a more objective lens. The lens from the space between worlds gives us a kind of objectivity not attainable from within the belief system of our culture. When we are dreaming at night, quite literally, there is no culture...no society and no rules. The space between Edison's hand and the rattling pie plate below knows no societal convention. It's the space of stardust; pure creativity; pure invention. If we try changing a failing system inside the language of our culture, it will not happen. Just like we cannot change ourselves using the language that is heavily marinated in our own beliefs. As it now is, we're actors in someone else's dream that simply no longer works.

That is what innocence really is in my eyes: the inner knowing and inner connectedness we are all born with. Animals live by it. Innocence is where there is no perception distortion and where we have a grounded and matter-of-fact knowing that all is as it should be.

I know

and

It's simple

You don't need to sell your house and all your possessions to know that you are not the sum total of everything you believe; everything you were taught; everything you own; everything you think you are.

From the altered reality of Edison's clattering pie plate.

From the place of wonder sweeping across the face of the young boy as he traces the random flight of a dragonfly.

From the place of hysterical laughter.

From the place of uncontrollable tears.

From the space within our daydreams:

From innocence.

We are that small group of thoughtful, committed citizens reclaiming our birth-right. We are not the babies on conveyor belts or society's 'sheeple'. We are innocents...separate and apart from the twisting and twirling madness of the duality of our culture. We are the 'other' as the two opposite qualities converge to create something transcendent and apart. It's from this place that we can order up a new recipe for humankind. A new script. A duality with the added missing ingredient: a harmonizing, transcendent and innocent mediator.

To be innocent again, I use the one miraculous thing I have, my will. With my will I can employ the inner lawyer/scientist/researcher to slowly, systematically and deliberately use the same mental inertia that originally dreamed up my persona and make up something else. Even the incomparably cunning limbic brain has no place to hide from my researchers. I am able to rout out even the most cunning belief. If I didn't think I could do it or *we* could do it, I wouldn't have risked every thing I know and own. And I know that conditioning the mind can work. I see politicians doing it all the time. I've seen a politician lie about something and repeat it so many times, that he finally believes his own lie. Completely. As if it is an absolute truth. And he'll fight to the death to defend it. And this is by simple dint of repetition and convincing the mind. If a politician can do it, so can I– but in *reverse*. I take the lie and alchemize it into a truth. Letting the brain know who's boss, I take the self-effacing untruth and simply replace it with an idea that feels good and true to me: The truth of who I am:

Innocent of being born into sin.

Innocent of wrong-doing.

Innocence is the place from which we love, we create, we dream and we imagine a world that has enough for all of us.

Looking back over my life, it was a pivotal moment when I decided to no longer talk about my love of classical music to my fifth grade class. I think we've all had a defining moment when we allowed the crush of peer pressure to override our better judgment. The other kids convinced me to go with the social current. That current carried me through the better part of my life. Fed by my own misinformation about my unworthiness, I now see that flow as a purposely designed tool of social engineering for someone else's prosperity and fulfillment – not mine.

Travel

I've always loved to travel. I've done a lot of it. And what I find from culture to culture is that each society and each social system makes up their own rules when faced with creating a society that functions. In one country you can walk down a street smiling at everyone you make eye contact with and have the smile come back to you, often several times over. Do the same thing in another country, or sometimes even a different town in the same country, and your smile seems to go unnoticed and people might even pretend they can't see you. The story of what life is in India is very different to what the story of what life is in Sweden. Every inveterate traveler knows this. Travelers seem to be experiencing a purer version of life by not being confined to the lens of a single social system. Realities are negotiable, create-able and malleable. Nowhere is this more obvious than in traveling. Flitting from one social system to another, the whole idea of social acceptability seems like something made up – something to suit the respective environment and individual needs of the people. Traveling is like skirting the societal veil. Wonderfully, that veil thins in developing countries. In places like Bali, Laos, Mexico and others, mothers have an innate trust of their *own* child-rearing ability so as to not put the 'authoritative' advice of experts or behaviorists above their own maternal instincts. Because of this, the children I've seen in these countries have an easiness about them. Without apology or self-consciousness, they seem to simply enjoy themselves. Their goal is not to be happy. They *are* happy. And sadly, many of *us* are not. We tend to put happiness off for the "Golden Years" – the mythical future time when we'd probably be too addled and feeble to enjoy it anyway.

I personally don't understand why anyone would choose to live in a place where people don't smile when you greet them with "hello". If a returned smile is that dangerous a thing to do, how could living in a place like that be a pleasurable experience? Living in a place where we need to be so cautious; so defended and so protective isn't the kind of place I'd want to live in, anyway.

Every Cell

In 1994, I was enthralled with the idea that there is actually very little matter in the universe. I loved the research that seemed to suggest to the scientific community that there was a whole new world out there – the world of an energy universe. In my enthusiasm, I wrote a musical, in 1995, and these are part of the lyrics from one of the songs:

If we're 99.9 percent space

Then there's very little left of us that's matter

if a thought can put a smile on your face

then a thought that you're fat can make you fatter

If you think it; it is so

so it's very good to know

that your mind is in control of all you see

So I'm justified to say

where there's a will there is a way

and what you will ...is what is going to be

I thought if everything in the known world: all matter, thoughts etc., was *energy*, that would really change my world view, so I conducted an experiment with myself around that same time:

I pictured each of the cells of my body as my children. I decided that I would care for these children so I simply sent them loving thoughts. When a negative thought, criticism or judgment would arise during the day, I'd replace that thought with a positive thought. Knowing that children can't distinguish between a negative thought directed outward and a negative thought directed inward, I kept them safe from any form of negativity. I tried not judging anyone; criticizing anyone or having even the remotest negative idea because I knew my cells would think it was their fault. That's what children do.

People noticed the change in me and asked what I was up to.

I promptly forgot about the experiment until just recently – 18 years later. I've started to love all my cells again by saying:

> I love you, my children.

Repeating the words over and over works wonders.

Try it.

Try it now.

These 30+ trillion cells all have awareness; a respiratory system, an elimination system – basically, they have everything we have. They are aware of themselves and each other. So, quite literally they ARE little people in community. When I send them love with a focused pure intent, I feel a response. For me, this is not at all an imagined response (which would be great too), but a palpable and sweet flooding of love coming right back to me. When this current really gets moving, I feel like I'm at the center of a free-energy machine.

This process reminds me of the theme of my talks with *actual* children when I was touring as the environmental spokesperson:

> "How long can you live without food?" I'd ask as hands
> would fly into the air.

Most of them could barely make it to lunch time without feeling faint so they were surprised to find out that we can live several months, without food, which they considered astounding.

> "Annnnd, how long can a person live without water?" I'd
> ask.

> "Two to three days or so," I'd reply after getting answers as
> off beat as 'several years'.

> "And, how long could you live without air? OK. Let me
> put it this way: how long can you hold your breath?"

They'd all immediately try it out as I'd hear coughs, grunts and sputters all around the room.

> "Probably only about 3-4 minutes. Now, wouldn't you say that air, food and water are 3 rather important things in our lives? And isn't it just amazing that this planet gives us the 3 things we just happen to need in order to survive. It's like the Earth is saying 'thanks for being here.' Often, though, we take air, food and water for granted. But these precious gifts, given to us by our planet, need to remain clean so we can stay healthy. There are many things we can do to keep air, food and water clean. It's one of the ways we can say 'thank you'. Thank you for giving me life. Can you tell me some other things we might be able to do to return the favor...to love our planet right back?"

The way I looked at it was, if I could make clear to just one kid that there is an important relationship between our health and the health of our planet, my job was done. Once an ambassador to the earth, always an ambassador to the earth. Within the idea of a "circle of kindness" was the formula to engineer and insure their own survival. That: loving creates survival and healthfulness.

Some unknown part of myself had been teaching me better than any instructor or book. Because, what I didn't know at the time was, not unlike with all the recordings I did for "children", I was teaching myself an important lesson: my relationships are all important. If I could create a "circle of kindness" with my own cells, I could stimulate and awaken an awareness of all the "circles of kindness".

In sending love to my cells, seeing them as innocent children, I am feeling that love coming back to me.

> Are these the "children" in the prescient dream I had when I was nothing more than a child myself at the time? The dream where I was collecting babies and placing them in the pram. This was the dream that created a sense of well-being that I hadn't had before or since.

As the exchange becomes a habit and a way of life, I am changed. I become a love-generator. What is more, that doorway as with all doorways, stimulates the exploration of *more love* and the discovery of more doorways. If I see myself as a cell among a community of cells on this organism we call our planet, what is to keep me then from doing the same thing with all my earth-community cells? If I send love to all people with whom I am, globally, in community – does the love come back? I'd say yes. Axiomatically, we can see our planet as a cell in an even greater cosmology of inter-galactic intelligent systems. And so on down to the smallest of particles. If it's all energy and space, well, there is no separation between the smallest intelligently operating particle and the largest intelligent system. Looked at this way there are no boundaries; there is no time or space. It's all one pulsing love system.

~

As of now, I'm drifting without any particular identity of being a salesman, or instructor or musician. And I feel like I'm more, not less. I feel like the world of all possibility opens up as I drop all things attached to my persona. No mental filters emerge in what I choose to do. I am light as a feather. I am not weighted by things that lock me into an image of myself. I am nothing. And all things. I am fixed on the space between worlds. The doorway.

That said, I have asked myself many times: "Can I do this?" Can I live without the headaches that seem to, by definition, accompany all that living in a "civilized" culture entails? Is living with an indigenous tribal people the only way to do it (as if they'd let me)? Because, let's face it, adult innocence and living in a first world country in the 21st century would not appear to go together. How can I live inside innocence in a world that seems anything *but* innocent? When stress, grief, drama, conformist pressures and my ego keep me estranged from this, my basic and original nature embodied in:

Watching dragonflies with the kind of wonder that makes everything else disappear.

Beholding the mystical moon as if it is about to impart to me the secrets within it.

Loving openly and without apology.

Maybe I knew the answer to this question when I was crawling around on the floor. I knew when the ancient sound of "ooom" came tumbling out of my one-year-old mouth foretelling something that wouldn't even occur to me until my early sixties.

A rOoom inside my awareness. Ooom. A rOoom in which the altar of my innocence remains untarnished and unmoved by the tides of Maya. The wOoomb of the Vesica Piscis in the space between opposites. Here, in this room is a part of me that is profoundly and intimately my own. A room from where springs my creativity. A room, inside which, meditation unfolds as the most natural and effortless thing to do. A room in which dreams are made. A room inside which lives an innocence, unlike the innocence of childhood, that can *never be taken away*; never be subverted by anything external be it conformist pressures, belief systems, trauma or anything setting out to sway my attention from my most precious of all gifts. And this is the grandest of differences between a child's innocence and an adult's reclaimed innocence:

No one. No thing. Can take it away. Because it was placed there consciously.

Within the room, I can still live side-by-side with the social monolith. This is the monolith constructed of belief systems; absolute certainties, the pain and suffering of man; the duality that is so much a part of the human experience; the never-ending stream of cars, and trains and planes all headed somewhere. If our profound ignorance, simply borne of bad habits, continues, it will always summon us back to war, conflict, greed and fear. In fact, from the perspective of my rOoom, societal contrivance can be looked upon like dragonflies hovering, then darting overhead. I can observe the whole spectacle with fascination again because it is wondrous and exciting to behold.

Living in the room of reclaimed innocence next to the cultural monolith, it all becomes playful again. It becomes do-able. It becomes sane.

And thanks to this room fashioned from dreams, meditation, Brahms, being still, and the knowing that I am not what I think I am,

I am almost innocent.

Meditation

Before your first email

Before your first argument at work

Before your first job

Before your first savings account

Before your first breakup

Before you ever went to school

Before anyone told you that you couldn't dance...or sing...or scream

Before your first loss

Before your first disappointment

Before you were ever shamed

Before your awareness of being in your family

Before your thoughts about who you were

Before your first concern

Before your first awareness...

...There was the miracle. The miracle of all that was wondrous. All that was amazing.

And you were at the center of it.

This is your home. This is what innocence is.

ABOUT MICHAEL MISH

Children's recording artist and public speaker,
Michael continues his travels in Australia and South East Asia
doing under-water video and interviewing children.

Other books by Michael Mish:
Maya and the Gordian Knot - Michael Mish & Jennifer Schloming
MGK Publishers

The Magic Stone - Dramatic Publishing
Teensomething - Eldridge Press

Other sites for Michael Mish include:
www.MichaelMishMusic.com
www.aKidsEyeView.com
www.MichaelMish.com

www.almost-innocent.com

Contact: info@almost-innocent.com
Published by Vesica Media 2012

photo by Shannon Jankula

Contents

Part 2

MICHAEL MISH

Index

A

B

C

I

J

K

L

M

www.ingramcontent.com/pod-product-compliance
Lightning Source LLC
Chambersburg PA
CBHW061142040426
42445CB00013B/1516